Baptism In the Holy Spirit

Kenneth E. Hagin

Unless otherwise indicated, all Scripture quotations in this volume are from the *King James Version* of the Bible.

First Printing 1998

ISBN 0-89276-063-X

In the U.S. write:
Kenneth Hagin Min-
istries
P.O. Box 50126
Tulsa, OK 74150-0126

In Canada write:
Kenneth Hagin Ministries
P.O. Box 335, Station D,
Etobicoke (Toronto), Ontario
Canada, M9A 4X3

Contents

Contents

The Baptism in the Holy Spirit — An Experience Subsequent to Salvation

Bible Text: Acts 8:12-19

Central Truth: There is an experience following salvation of being filled with the Holy Spirit.

As a young denominational minister, I had been taught that when a person is saved, he *has* the Holy Spirit — which is true in a sense. However, my denomination taught that when one is saved, he has *all* of the Holy Spirit it is possible to have.

The Scripture passage below helped me see that there is an experience subsequent to salvation called receiving the Holy Spirit, or the baptism in the Holy Spirit.

These verses show that although the Samaritans were saved, the apostles didn't seem to think they had all of the Holy Spirit it is possible to have.

Philip's Ministry In Samaria

ACTS 8:12,13
12 But when they believed Philip preaching the things concerning the kingdom of God, and the name of Jesus Christ, they were baptized, both men and women.
13 Then Simon himself believed also: and when he was baptized, he continued with Philip, and wondered, beholding the miracles and signs which were done.

Philip's ministry in Samaria was abundantly blessed of God. Mighty miracles constantly were being performed. Many were saved and healed, according to Acts 8:7,8: *"For unclean spirits, crying with loud voice, came out of many that were possessed with them: and many taken with palsies, and that were lame, were healed. And there was great joy in that city."*

The Samaritans believed Philip's sermons concerning the Kingdom of God and the Name of Jesus, and they

1

were baptized in water: *"But when they BELIEVED Philip preaching the things concerning the kingdom of God, and the name of Jesus Christ, they were BAPTIZED, both men and women"* (v. 12).

Jesus had said, *"... Go ye into all the world and preach the gospel to every creature. He that BELIEVETH and is BAPTIZED shall be saved..."* (Mark 16:15). These Samaritans both believed and were baptized. Were they saved? According to Jesus they were! Yet none of them had received the baptism in the Holy Spirit.

There is a work of the Holy Spirit involved in the *New Birth*, but that work is not called receiving the Holy Spirit (or the baptism in the Holy Spirit). It is called being *born again* (or receiving eternal life). The experience that follows salvation is called *receiving the Holy Spirit, the baptism in the Holy Spirit, or being filled with the Holy Spirit*.

We are born again by the Word of God. Peter says we are born *"not of corruptible seed, but of incorruptible, BY THE WORD OF GOD, which liveth and abideth for ever"* (1 Peter 1:23).

Peter and John Sent to Samaria

ACTS 8:14-17
14 Now when the apostles which were at Jerusalem heard that Samaria had received the word of God, they sent unto them Peter and John:
15 Who, when they were come down, prayed for them, that they might receive the Holy Ghost:
16 (For as yet he was fallen upon none of them: only they were baptized in the name of the Lord Jesus.)
17 Then laid they their hands on them, and they received the Holy Ghost.

Our text in verse fourteen says, *"Now when the apostles which were at Jerusalem heard that Samaria HAD RECEIVED THE WORD OF GOD...."* This is conclusive proof that these people were genuinely saved. The apostles recognized they were saved, because after they heard of the wonderful things God had done through Philip's ministry, they sent Peter and John to lay hands on the new converts that they might receive the Holy Spirit.

There is no record that any upon whom Peter and John laid hands failed to receive. The Bible simply states, *"Then laid they their hands on them, and they received the Holy Ghost"* (Acts 8:17).

Peter and John were sent to Samaria for a specific purpose. What was this purpose? The answer is found in verse fifteen: *"Who, when they were come down, prayed for them, that they might receive the Holy Ghost."*

The other apostles in Jerusalem sent them to Samaria for this specific purpose. Why did they have to pray for those Samaritans to receive the Holy Spirit? Why couldn't Philip have prayed for them just as well?

We must remember we all have our place in God's plan. We must find that place and do what God wants us to do. God has special ministries; He didn't call all of us to minister the same, and He didn't give all of us the same ministry.

Philip was an evangelist. His ministry was leading many to an experience of salvation in Jesus Christ. Peter and John, on the other hand, had a specific ministry of laying hands on people to receive the baptism in the Holy Spirit.

Simon the Sorcerer

ACTS 8:18,19

18 And when Simon saw that through laying on of the apostles' hands the Holy Ghost was given, he offered them money,

19 Saying, Give me also this power, that on whomsoever I lay hands, he may receive the Holy Ghost.

Simon the sorcerer offered Peter and John money, saying, ". . . *Give me also this power, that on whomsoever I lay hands, he may receive the Holy Ghost*" (v. 19).

Some have thought Simon tried to buy the Holy Spirit. He didn't. He tried to buy the *ability* to lay hands on people and have them receive the Holy Spirit.

Peter answered him, ". . .*Thy money perish with thee, because thou hast thought that the gift of God may be purchased with money*" (v. 20).

There are four different Greek words translated "gift" in the New Testament. This particular Greek word means "an endowment." Peter said he and John were endowed, or gifted, by the Holy Spirit to lay hands on people to receive the baptism of the Holy Spirit.

How do we know these Samaritans actually spoke in tongues? Some who do not believe in tongues argue that this scripture says nothing about their speaking in tongues.

There is no evidence, however, that they did *not* speak with tongues. In fact, students of Church history know the Early Church fathers agree that they did speak with tongues in Samaria. And we read elsewhere in the New Testament that those who were filled with the Holy Spirit spoke with tongues.

Also it is apparent that these Samaritans must have spoken in tongues, because ". . . *Simon SAW that through laying on of the apostles' hands the Holy Ghost was given . . .*" (v. 18).

Certainly the Holy Spirit cannot be seen with the physical eye, because He is a Spirit. Yet there had to be some kind of physical sign whereby Simon knew they had received the Holy Spirit. There had to have been something that registered on Simon's physical senses so he could tell that they had received the Holy Spirit. Simon didn't receive the Holy Spirit himself, but he could see that the others had. How?

"Maybe it was because Simon saw the Samaritans were full of joy," one minister said to me. This, however, couldn't explain it, because Simon already had seen their joy. Verse eight reports, ". . . *there was great joy in that city.*" They already had joy *before* Peter and John arrived from Jerusalem, and *before* they received the baptism of the Holy Spirit.

What kind of sign, then, would cause Simon to know these people had received the Holy Spirit when Peter and John laid hands on them? All evidence indicates that the sign which was manifested was speaking in tongues. That was the sign that convinced Simon they had received the Holy Spirit.

Speaking in tongues is not the Holy Spirit, and the Holy Spirit is not speaking in tongues — but they go hand in hand. It's like the tongue in the shoe. The tongue isn't the shoe, and the shoe isn't the tongue, but each is an important part of the other.

When somebody buys an automobile in Texas, he is issued a certificate of title as evidence of ownership. The automobile is not the certificate of title, and the title is not the automobile, but you'll not get very far in that automobile without the certificate (or evidence) of title.

If you have the infilling of the Holy Spirit, you should have the *evidence* (tongues) to go along with it.

Notice there is not the least suggestion in Acts 8 that Peter and John taught the Samaritans to tarry (or wait) for the Holy Spirit.

To teach people to tarry for the infilling of the Holy Spirit, which already has been given as a free gift, only produces doubt and indecision.

Howard Carter, who was general supervisor of the Assemblies of God in Great Britain for many years, founded the oldest Pentecostal Bible school in the world, and he was a leading teacher in Full Gospel circles around the world. He said that to teach people to wait for the Holy Spirit is nothing but a combination of works and unbelief.

A Free Gift

Notice something else in Acts 8: Peter and John did not pray that

God would *give* the Samaritans the Holy Spirit. They prayed that the Samaritans would *receive* the Holy Spirit.

Often we pray, "Lord, save souls at this service tonight. Heal the sick." However, we do not find where they ever prayed that way in the Acts of the Apostles (and we should pray according to the Word).

I pray for people, but not that God would save them, because He already has done something about saving them: He sent His Son to die for us. God already has purchased salvation for each man; however, it is not going to do us any good until we accept it. That is the reason He told us to spread the Good News.

Scripturally, we should pray that people will *receive* the gift of eternal life that is offered to them.

I don't pray that God would fill people with the Holy Spirit. I pray like Peter and John did, that they might *receive* the gift God offers.

Also notice that the seventeenth verse of this passage does not say, "Then laid they their hands on them and God filled them with the Holy Ghost." It says, ". . . *and they RECEIVED the Holy Ghost.*"

I believe we are in good company with Peter and John, so I follow the same procedure they followed: I lay hands on people to receive the Holy Spirit. I do it in faith because it is scriptural. I also do it because I have a ministry along that line. The apostles sent Peter and John to Samaria because they had a ministry along this line. (God anoints us to minister according to His calling on our lives.)

As a denominational pastor half a century ago, when I read the New Testament and the Spirit of God enlightened me on these verses, I was convinced that if I received the same Holy Spirit they had received, I would have the same initial sign of speaking with tongues. I wasn't satisfied with anything less.

Memory Text:
"For John truly baptized with water; but ye shall be baptized with the Holy Ghost not many days hence."
—Acts 1:5

The Promise and Its Fulfillment

Bible Texts: John 14:16,17; Acts 2:32,33;
John 4:13,14; 7:37-39

Central Truth: The Lord has promised "rivers of living water" to quench man's spiritual thirst.

In the verses below we see Jesus' promise of the gift of the Holy Spirit. Then in Acts 2 we see the fulfillment of that promise.

JOHN 14:16,17
16 And I will pray the Father, and he shall give you another Comforter, that he may abide with you for ever;
17 Even the Spirit of truth; whom the world cannot receive, because it seeth him not, neither knoweth him: but ye know him; for he dwelleth with you, and shall be in you.

ACTS 2:32,33
32 This Jesus hath God raised up, whereof we all are witnesses.
33 Therefore being by the right hand Of God exalted, and having received of the Father the promise of the Holy Ghost, he hath shed forth this, which ye now see and hear.

The Promised Comforter

Jesus prayed that the Father would send another Comforter to abide forever. Then on the Day of Pentecost He shed forth the Holy Spirit, who has been here ever since. It is now not a matter of the Father's *giving* anyone the Holy Spirit. It is a matter of our *receiving* the Holy Spirit.

Notice Jesus' words, *"I will pray the Father, and he shall give you another Comforter, that HE may abide with you for ever."* When we receive the Holy Spirit, we receive "Him," not "it." We have heard people say, "I received the baptism." However, they didn't receive the baptism; they received the Holy Spirit.

Others say, "I am filled with the baptism." They are not filled with the baptism. They are not even filled with the baptism in the Holy Spirit. They are filled with the Holy Spirit, the Third Person of the Godhead.

Receiving the Holy Spirit is more than an experience: A divine Personality comes to live in us — to dwell in us — to make His home in us.

We must not be so concerned with an outward experience that we miss the reality of the indwelling presence of the Holy Spirit. If we have been filled with the Holy Spirit, we should be conscious of His presence every waking moment. We shouldn't have to look back to some experience we had at an altar years ago. The Holy Spirit should become more real and precious to us every day!

The Promise Is for Believers

Notice also that the infilling of the Holy Spirit is not for sinners; it is for believers. Referring to the infilling of the Holy Spirit, Jesus said, *"Even the Spirit of truth, whom the world cannot receive."*

The world can receive eternal life: *"For God so loved the WORLD, that he gave his only begotten Son, that whosoever believeth in him should not perish, but have everlasting life"* (John 3:16). The world can receive Christ as Savior — the world can be born again — but a person must be born again *before* he can receive the infilling of the Holy Spirit.

To illustrate this, Jesus said in Matthew 9:17, *"Neither do men put new wine into old bottles: else the bottles break, and the wine runneth out . . . they put new wine into new bottles . . ."* (In those days wine was stored in skin bottles.)

In the Scriptures, wine is a type of the Holy Spirit. Jesus was therefore saying that the Holy Spirit could not be given in His fullness unless one had been made a new creature. Otherwise, as Jesus pointed out, if you were to put new wine in old bottles, they would burst. If He put the Holy Spirit in people who had not been born again, they would burst. *"Therefore if any man be in Christ, he is a new creature . . ."* (2 Cor. 5:17).

When you have been made a new creature, you are ready to be filled with the new wine.

Also referring to the Holy Spirit, Jesus said in Luke 11:13, *"If ye then, being evil, know how to give good gifts unto your children: how much more shall your heavenly Father give the Holy Spirit to them that ask him?"*

God isn't the Father of everyone. We hear a lot these days about the Fatherhood of God and the brotherhood of man, and that God is the Father of all of us and we are all brothers. That isn't true. Jesus told the Pharisees, the strictest sect of the Jewish religion, *"Ye are of your father the devil . . ."* (John 8:44). God

8

is the Father only of those who have been born again. And for those who have been born again, the Father has for them the gift of the infilling of the Holy Spirit.

Come and Drink

JOHN 4:13,14
13 Jesus answered and said unto her, Whosoever drinketh of this water shall thirst again:
14 But whosoever drinketh of the water that I shall give him shall never thirst; but the water that I shall give him shall be in him a well of water springing up into everlasting life.

JOHN 7:37-39
37 In the last day, the great day of the feast, Jesus stood and cried, saying, If any man thirst, let him come unto me, and drink.
38 He that believeth on me, as the scripture hath said, out of his belly shall flow rivers of living water.
39 (But this spake he of the Spirit, which they that believe on him should receive: for the Holy Ghost was not yet given; because that Jesus was not yet glorified.)

The water referred to in both passages above is a type of the Holy Spirit. Notice that two *different* experiences are spoken of.

First, to the woman at the well of Samaria Jesus said, *"But the water that I shall give him shall be in him a well of water springing up into*

everlasting life." Here Jesus was referring to the Holy Spirit in the act of *regeneration* or *salvation.* (The Holy Spirit is represented as a "well of water springing up into everlasting life.")

The other reference is to "rivers of living water," and speaks of the promise of *the infilling of the Holy Spirit: "Out of his belly* [innermost being] *shall flow rivers of living water."*

Jesus beckons us to come and drink and get full. "But how can you know when you get full?" someone may ask. For the answer, let us look at Acts 2:4: *"And they were all filled with the Holy Ghost, and began to speak with other tongues, as the Spirit gave them utterance."*

If you are a believer, it is just as simple as Jesus said it is. Come and drink, and keep drinking until you get full! When you get full, you will start speaking with other tongues. This is the initial sign or evidence that you are filled.

✳

Memory Text:
" ... If any man thirst, let him come unto me, and drink."
— John 7:37

The Holy Spirit — An Ever Present Source of Power

Bible Texts: 1 Corinthians 3:16; 6:19; 2 Corinthians 6:16

Central Truth: Every Spirit-filled believer has within him all the power he will ever need to put him over in this life.

The New Testament gives us three relations that God sustains toward man: (1) God *for* us; (2) God *with* us; (3) God *in* us.

To have God *for* us guarantees success: *"If God be for us, who can be against us?"* (Rom. 8:31). If God is on our side, we are sure to win. If God is *for* us — and we know He is for us — we become utterly fearless in life. No matter how difficult the situation may be — no matter how dark the clouds may hang upon the horizon of our life — we are calmly assured that we must win. There can be no defeat if the Lord is for us.

We can also have the assurance that God is with us. No matter what the circumstances may be, our Lord is with us. The knowledge of the Word of God along this line should certainly cause our hearts to leap

within us for joy and buoy our spirits up in faith and confidence.

In the New Testament we have *"a better covenant, which was established upon better promises"* (Heb. 8:6). Under the covenant in the Old Testament, God was for Israel and was with Israel, but He was not *in* them.

God is for us and with us today, but we also have something better: God is *in* us. God is actually making His home *in* our bodies!

Our Bodies the Temple of God

1 CORINTHIANS 3:16

16 Know ye not that ye are the temple of God, and that the Spirit of God dwelleth in you?

1 CORINTHIANS 6:19

19 What? know ye not that your body is the temple of the Holy Ghost

11

which is in you, which ye have of God, and ye are not your own?

2 CORINTHIANS 6:16
16 And what agreement hath the temple of God with idols? for ye are the temple of the living God; as God hath said, I will dwell in them, and walk in them; and I will be their God, and they shall be my people.

Too few of us are really conscious of God in our bodies. If men and women were conscious of God in their bodies, they wouldn't talk and act as they do. Some Christians constantly talk about their lack of power; their lack of ability. If they realized that God is in them, they would know that nothing is impossible to them!

The Bible says, "... *all things are possible to him that believeth*" (Mark 9:23). The reason all things are possible to him that believeth is because God our Father planned that the believer should have God Himself living in him through the power of the Holy Spirit. And with God in a person, nothing is impossible.

Of all the mighty truths connected with our redemption, this is the climax: *After God Himself has recreated us and made us new creatures — made us His own — then He, in the Person of the Holy Spirit, makes our bodies His home.*

John wrote in his first Epistle, "*Ye are of God, little children, and have*

overcome them: because greater is he that is in you, than he that is in the world" (1 John 4:4).

Both Paul and John were writing to people who not only had received eternal life, but were Spirit-filled believers — those in whom the Holy Spirit had come to dwell — those who had the supernatural sign or witness of His indwelling presence: speaking with other tongues.

John said, "*. . . greater is he that is in you, than he that is in the world.*" *I maintain that every born-again, Spirit-filled believer has within him, ready to use, all the power he will ever need to put him over in this life.*

When we put the scriptures quoted above together, it is quite obvious that through the infilling of the Holy Spirit, the Third Person of the Godhead — God Himself — indwells the believer. No longer does He dwell in a man-made Holy of Holies. Our bodies have become His temple.

Old Covenant Finished

In the Old Testament, under the Old Covenant, God's presence was kept enclosed in the Holy of Holies. No one dared approach that place except the High Priest, and he only with great precautions. If anyone else dared to intrude, he fell dead. It was necessary for every male throughout Israel to present himself at least once a year at Jerusalem, because that was where God's Presence was.

But just before Jesus died on the cross, He said, "It is finished." He was not referring to the New Covenant; He was talking about the Old Covenant. The New Covenant was not finished until Christ ascended on High and entered into the heavenly Holy of Holies with His own blood to obtain eternal redemption for us, as Hebrews declares. Then and only then was the New Covenant finished.

When Jesus, on Golgotha's rugged hill, said, "It is finished," the Bible tells us that the curtain that partitioned off the Holy of Holies in the Temple was rent in two from top to bottom.

Josephus, the Jewish historian, tells us this curtain was forty feet across, twenty feet high, and four inches thick. God sent His messenger down there to rend that curtain apart from top to bottom, signifying that the Old Covenant was finished.

God's Presence, which had been contained in the Holy of Holies, left that man-made structure. He has never again dwelled in a man-made building.

When we call a building "the house of God," we are partly correct and partly incorrect, according to what we mean by it. If we mean the building is a house of God because God lives and dwells there, we are wrong. *He does not dwell in a building.*

If we mean that it is God's house and is sacred because it is built in the Name of Jesus and is dedicated to the service of the Lord, then we are correct — it is a house of God. However, God doesn't *live* in a building made with hands; He lives and dwells in us through the power of the Holy Spirit.

John said, "*. . . greater is he that is in you. . . .*" Looking again at John 14:16 (which we studied in our last lesson), Jesus said, *"And I will pray the Father, and he shall give you another Comforter, that he may abide with you for ever."* And at the end of the seventeenth verse, *"He. . . shall be in you."* That is what John is saying too, as he writes to born-again, Spirit-filled believers: *"Greater is he that is in you, than he that is in the world."* Who is "he that is in the world"? Satan, the god of this world.

But He who is in you is greater. If we were conscious of the Greater One in us, we would have no fear of the devil, because He who is in us is greater than he who is in the world.

If we are conscious of the Greater One who indwells us and we believe what the Word of God says about His presence, no matter what or whom we face, we will have no fear. We have the Source of all power dwelling in us.

As the Holy Spirit dwells within us, according to Christ's promise, we will walk in the power of the Holy Spirit. We do not have to be defeated by the circumstances of life. We can rise above our physical limitations through the power of His Spirit.

Memory Text:
"... *greater is he that is in you, than he that is in the world.*"
— 1 John 4:4

The Evidence of the Holy Spirit's Indwelling

Bible Texts: Acts 10:44-46; 11:15-18; 19:1-6

Central Truth: Speaking in tongues is the physical evidence of a spiritual experience.

In Acts 10, we see an example of the manifestation of tongues being the convincing proof that believers had received the Holy Spirit.

ACTS 10:44-46

44 While Peter yet spake these words, the Holy Ghost fell on all them which heard the word.

45 And they of the circumcision which believed were astonished, as many as came with Peter, because that on the Gentiles also was poured out the gift of the Holy Ghost.

46 For they heard them speak with tongues, and magnify God.

After Peter's dramatic vision of the sheet filled with all manner of unclean beasts being let down from heaven, he was summoned to the house of Cornelius, a Gentile, to pro-

claim God's salvation through Jesus Christ.

As Peter spoke to Cornelius and his household concerning the remission of sins through the blood of Jesus, the Holy Spirit fell on all of them and they spoke with other tongues.

When the Jewish brethren at Jerusalem heard that Peter had carried the Gospel to Gentiles, they were highly critical and said, *". . . Thou wentest in to men uncircumcised, and didst eat with them"* (Acts 11:3).

Then Peter told them in detail about the vision the Lord had given him, admonishing him, *". . . What God hath cleansed, that call not thou common"* (v 9). Peter then presented evidence proving the Gentiles' salvation was genuine and therefore ought to be recognized by the Jewish brethren.

ACTS 11:15-18

15 And as I [Peter] began to speak, the Holy Ghost fell on them, as on us at the beginning.
16 Then remembered I the word of the Lord, how that he said, John indeed baptized with water; but ye shall be baptized with the Holy Ghost.
17 Forasmuch then as God gave them the like gift as he did unto us, who believed on the Lord Jesus Christ; what was I, that I could withstand God?
18 When they [the Jewish brethren] heard these things, they held their peace, and glorified God, saying, Then hath God also to the Gentiles granted repentance unto life.

Notice that it was *speaking in tongues* which finally convinced the group that accompanied Peter to Cornelius' house (as well as the Jewish Christians at Jerusalem) that these Gentiles had received the gift of salvation.

It also is interesting to note that they received salvation and the baptism of the Holy Spirit almost simultaneously. (When a person is first saved, that is the best time to get him or her filled with the Holy Spirit.) No one had laid hands on these Gentiles. They had all received

the Holy Spirit at about the same time. None failed to receive.

Here again we see no suggestion that they tarried or waited to be filled with the Holy Spirit.

The Holy Spirit Outpoured at Ephesus

ACTS 19:1-6

1 And it came to pass, that, while Apollos was at Corinth, Paul having passed through the upper coasts came to Ephesus: and finding certain disciples,
2 He said unto them, Have ye received the Holy Ghost since ye believed? And they said unto him, We have not so much as heard whether there be any Holy Ghost.
3 And he said unto them, Unto what then were ye baptized? And they said, Unto John's baptism.
4 Then said Paul, John verily baptized with the baptism of repentance, saying unto the people, that they should believe on him which should come after him, that is, on Christ Jesus.
5 When they heard this, they were baptized in the name of the Lord Jesus.
6 And when Paul had laid his hands upon them, the Holy Ghost came on them; and they spake with tongues, and prophesied.

Here we see another example of Gentiles receiving the infilling of the Holy Spirit. These men were all new converts who had been followers of

John the Baptist. They had heard John preach that the Promised One was coming. They had believed John's message, and they had been baptized by him in the Name of the Father. However, because news didn't travel as fast then as it does now, they had not yet heard that the Promised One had come.

Then Paul came and told them that Jesus, the Promised One, had come, had died on the cross, and had been resurrected; and now they should believe on Him. Paul then baptized them in the Name of the Lord Jesus.

But he didn't stop there. He also wanted them to be filled with the Holy Spirit. When he laid his hands on them, *". . . the Holy Ghost came upon them, and they spake with tongues, and prophesied"* (v. 6).

Without exception, all these new converts received the Holy Spirit when Paul laid hands on them! Again, there was no suggestion of tarrying.

Notice also that they *"spake with tongues and prophesied."* Sometimes people receive an additional spiritual blessing in addition to tongues when they are filled with the Spirit, but tongues always comes first. (The scripture didn't say they prophesied and spoke with tongues; it said they spoke with tongues first and then prophesied.) I have seen people speak with tongues and prophesy when they received the Holy Spirit. I have also seen people speak with tongues and interpret when they received the Holy Spirit. We should expect to speak with tongues. If something else is added, well and good.

When I received the baptism in the Holy Spirit, I received a gift of the Spirit too, although I didn't realize it at the time. I knew I had received the Holy Spirit because I spoke with tongues, but to be perfectly honest, I felt a little disappointed. Having heard some Christians tell of their experiences when they were filled with the Holy Spirit, I expected to have some kind of overwhelming hilarious experience, but I didn't.

Afterwards, I said to myself, *All I did was talk in tongues. I've gotten a bigger blessing than this many times just praying.*

But the baptism in the Holy Spirit is not just receiving a blessing; it is much more. I knew my Bible, so I said, *I don't care what I feel or what I don't feel. I know I have received the Holy Spirit because I have spoken with other tongues. I have the Bible evidence.*

I continued to praise God in this manner for about three days. Later I realized that at the same time I had received the Holy Spirit and had spoken with tongues, I had received another gift of the Spirit — the word of knowledge.

The Door into the Spiritual Gifts

As we have seen, speaking with tongues is the initial, supernatural sign or evidence of the Holy Spirit's indwelling. Speaking with tongues is the door into the spiritual gifts.

I have found in my own life that the more I pray and worship God in tongues, the more manifestations I have of the other gifts of the Spirit. The less I talk in tongues, the fewer manifestations I have.

Speaking with tongues is the door into all the rest of the spiritual gifts. Some people are only interested in the other gifts of the Spirit, but we have to go through the "door" to get there.

The Bible teaches us to be desirous of spiritual gifts (1 Cor. 14:1), and to covet earnestly the best gifts (1 Cor. 12:31). But remember that *those words were written to people who already spoke in tongues!* They weren't written to people who did not speak with tongues.

In the Corinthian church there was an abundance of speaking with tongues. In fact, it seemed that when they went to church, all of them wanted to speak with tongues at once! That isn't edifying, so Paul told

them that only two or three should speak in public, and another should interpret. And if an interpreter wasn't present, they should keep silent in the church (1 Cor. 14:27,28).

Paul didn't say they had the wrong thing. They had the right thing, but they were so thrilled and exuberant, they all wanted to talk at once. If everyone is praising God, it is all right for all to praise God in tongues at once. But it certainly would be wrong if everyone started talking in tongues while someone was trying to preach. Also, it would not be right for someone to spend an hour teaching in tongues without any interpretation. The speaker would be edified, but the listener wouldn't get anything out of it.

As Paul said, it is better to speak a few words with our own understanding so we can teach others than to speak ten thousand words in tongues unless there is an interpretation.

Some people, however, have made a mountain out of a molehill. They say that Paul was telling the Corinthians not to speak with tongues at all. This couldn't have been his intention, however, because he had just said, *"I thank my God, I speak with tongues more than ye all: Yet in the church I had rather speak five words with my understanding, that by my voice I might teach others also . . ."* (1 Cor. 14:18,19). Certainly it would be better for him to stand before the congregation and speak ten words in his own language so they could understand him than it would be to stand there and speak ten thousand words in tongues that were uninterpreted.

But in order to correct one error Paul did not suggest we make another by abandoning speaking in tongues altogether. Rather, we are told to covet earnestly the best gifts. As we do this and walk into a more powerful and effective Christian life, we will go through the door of the baptism in the Holy Spirit to receive the glorious spiritual gifts God has promised those who believe in His Word.

Memory Text:
"For they heard them speak with tongues, and magnify God."
— Acts 10:46

Is It Necessary To Speak in Tongues?

Bible Text: 1 Corinthians 13:8-12; 12:8-10,27-30

Central Truth: Many have been robbed of the blessing God has for them by believing that speaking in tongues isn't for everybody, or that it is one of the lesser gifts.

There is more to being filled with the Holy Spirit than speaking in tongues, but tongues are an integral and important part of receiving the Holy Spirit. Paul said, *"I thank my God, I speak with tongues . . ."* (1 Cor. 14:18).

Have Tongues Been Done Away With?

There are those who say, "Tongues have been done away with, because the Bible says that tongues have ceased." Let us look at the passage of Scripture that is used in connection with this argument.

1 CORINTHIANS 13:8-12

8 Charity never faileth: but whether there be prophecies, they shall fail; whether there be tongues, they shall cease; whether there be knowledge, it shall vanish away.
9 For we know in part, and we prophesy in part.
10 But when that which is perfect is come, then that which is in part shall be done away.
11 When I was a child, I spake as a child, I understood as a child, I thought as a child: but when I became a man, I put away childish things.
12 For now we see through a glass, darkly; but then face to face: now I know in part; but then shall I know even as also I am known.

Those who believe that tongues have been done away with say that the Bible is "that which is perfect" — and because we now have the Bible in its complete form, we no longer need supernatural gifts. Of course, the Bible is perfect, but our understanding of

God's Word is imperfect. Therefore, we still "see through a glass, darkly." This scripture says that when that which is perfect is come, we shall see face to face, and not through a glass darkly. Since it is quite evident that we still see through a glass darkly, it is also obvious that that which is perfect has not yet come.

Some say that tongues have ceased, but they don't say anything about knowledge having vanished away. Knowledge has not vanished. Prophecies have not failed. And tongues have not ceased.

One of these days, of course, tongues *will* cease. In heaven there will be no need for tongues. Paul stated, *"For he that speaketh in an unknown tongue speaketh not unto men, but unto God: for no man understandeth him; howbeit in the spirit he speaketh mysteries"* (1 Cor. 14:2). In James Moffatt's translation, he says that the speaker in tongues speaks "divine secrets" in the Spirit. When we get to heaven, there won't be any more mysteries or secrets, so it will not be necessary to speak with tongues. As long as we are this side of heaven, however, tongues will not cease.

Is It Necessary for All To Speak in Tongues?

Then there are those who profess to believe in tongues, but who do not believe that tongues are necessary for all Christians. They use the argument from First Corinthians 12:30: *"...do all speak with tongues?"* However, one could take part of a verse or even an entire verse of Scripture out of its setting and prove anything. We must read the entire passage to understand what it really means.

1 CORINTHIANS 12:27-30
27 Now ye are the body of Christ, and members in particular.
28 And God hath set some in the church, first apostles, secondarily prophets, thirdly teachers, after that miracles, then gifts of healings, helps, governments, diversities of tongues.
29 Are all apostles? are all prophets? are all teachers? are all workers of miracles?
30 Have all the gifts of healing? do all speak with tongues? do all interpret?

In verse twenty-eight Paul is talking about the *ministry gifts* that God has set in the Church. "Apostles" is not a spiritual gift, but an office, or a ministry gift. "Prophets" is not a spiritual gift, but a ministry gift. Likewise, "teachers" is not a spiritual gift, but a ministry gift to minister to the Body of Christ.

In the first part of this chapter, Paul does list spiritual gifts.

1 CORINTHIANS 12:8-10
8 For to one is given by the Spirit the word of wisdom; to another the

word of knowledge by the same Spirit;

9 To another faith by the same Spirit; to another the gifts of healing by the same Spirit;

10 To another the working of miracles; to another prophecy; to another discerning of spirits; to another divers kinds of tongues; to another the interpretation of tongues ....

It is certainly true that the gifts of the Spirit may be manifested through *laymen*, because Paul said, *"... the manifestation of the Spirit is given to EVERY MAN to profit withal"* (1 Cor. 12:7).

There are also those in the *ministry* who are equipped with the gifts of the Spirit. We do not call these people "spiritual gifts." As Paul says here, God has set ministries — five ministry gifts — in the Church.

In writing to the Church at Ephesus, Paul lists these gifts. He said that when Jesus ascended on high, *"He gave some, apostles; and some, prophets; and some, evangelists; and some, pastors and teachers"* (Eph. 4:11).

When Paul wrote to the Corinthians about these ministry gifts, we notice that neither the ministry of an evangelist nor a pastor is listed (1 Cor. 12:28). Since the pastor is head of the church, his ministry gift is included in the office of govern-

ments. The working of miracles and gifts of healings are included in the office of an evangelist.

Philip is a type of a New Testament evangelist. We read of him: *"Then Philip went down to the city of Samaria, and preached Christ unto them. And the people with one accord gave heed unto those things which Philip spake, hearing and seeing the miracles which he did. For unclean spirits, crying with loud voice, came out of many that were possessed with them: and many taken with palsies, and that were lame, were healed"* (Acts 8:5-7). Later, Philip was called an evangelist.

If a person is a New Testament evangelist, he is equipped with such supernatural gifts as working of miracles or gifts of healings. It takes these gifts to constitute his office. Many times we call people evangelists when they are really exhorters. (Paul speaks of exhorters in the Book of Romans.) Those who just exhort sinners to get saved — but have no working of gifts of healings or miracles or the supernatural in their lives — are not evangelists; they are exhorters.

As we have pointed out, Paul is speaking about a ministry gift of *diversities of tongues* in First Corinthians 12:29,30. He isn't talking about being filled with the Holy Spirit and speaking with tongues.

He asks, *"Are all apostles?* [No.] *are all prophets?* [No.] *are all teachers?* [No.] *are all workers of miracles?* [No.] *Have all the gifts of healings?"* [No.]

Then he asks, *"Do all speak with tongues? do all interpret?"* According to what he is talking about here, the answer is no. He is not talking about people being filled with the Holy Spirit and speaking with tongues. He is talking about *ministering tongues* in a public assembly with interpretation. Everyone doesn't do that!

Are Tongues Really Important?

Many believers have been robbed of the blessings God intended them to have because they believe that speaking in tongues isn't for everyone, or that speaking in tongues is one of the lesser gifts.

Early in my Christian walk, before I became aware that I didn't have any spiritual gifts at all, I can remember saying, "We've got wisdom and knowledge, and those are the greater gifts!"

What I didn't know was that Paul wasn't talking about intellectual wisdom and knowledge. The Scripture says, *"For to one is given by the Spirit the word of wisdom; to another the word of knowledge. . ."* (1 Cor. 12:8).

This is speaking of spiritual gifts: the *word of wisdom* and the *word of knowledge.*

But in my ignorance I said, "We have wisdom and knowledge. A few of those Pentecostals might have that little ole gift mentioned down at the bottom of the list — tongues — but that isn't very important. We don't need it." To my utter astonishment, the Spirit of God began to show me from His Word that I needed to be filled with the Holy Spirit, and that when I got filled, I would speak with tongues!

✳

Memory Text:

"And they were all filled with the Holy Ghost, and began to speak with other tongues, as the Spirit gave them utterance."

— Acts 2:4

24

What Purpose Do Tongues Serve?

Bible Texts: 1 Corinthians 14:2,4,13; Galatians 5:22,23

Central Truth: Speaking in tongues is a supernatural means of building ourselves up spiritually through communication with God.

In writing to the Church at Corinth, Paul strongly encourages believers to speak in tongues in their own private prayer lives, and he gives them several reasons for doing so:

1 CORINTHIANS 14:2,4,13
2 For he that speaketh in an unknown tongue speaketh not unto men, but unto God: for no man understandeth him; howbeit in the spirit he speaketh mysteries....
4 He that speaketh in an unknown tongue edifieth himself; but he that prophesieth edifieth the church....
13 Wherefore let him that speaketh in an unknown tongue pray that he may interpret.

The word "unknown" is italicized in the *King James* translation. When a word in the Bible is italicized, it means that word isn't in the original Scriptures; it was added by the translators to clarify the meaning. In one sense there is no such thing as an "unknown" tongue. The translators of the *King James Version* added the word "unknown" so the readers would know that the tongue is "unknown" to the one doing the speaking: He never learned it — it was imparted supernaturally. It isn't unknown to everyone, and it certainly isn't unknown to God.

For example, I have spoken a number of different languages unknown to me and which I never learned, such as Hebrew and Chinese. People present, who knew the language, understood what I said. However, if you were to ask me now to speak those languages, I wouldn't be able to say one word!

In fact, the impact of your speaking in an unknown tongue (unknown to you, but known to others) can even lead to someone's salvation, as in a situation I once encountered.

A Jewish man, who didn't believe in Christ or the New Testament, attended one of my services. At the close of my sermon, I spoke in tongues and interpreted. He came up to me afterwards and said, "I heard you speak in Aramaic tonight and then translate it." When I told him that I didn't know that language, he was astounded and asked how this could be. I explained that I was speaking with other tongues and interpreting the tongues as the Bible states in First Corinthians 14:13: *"Wherefore let him that speaketh in an unknown tongue pray that he may interpret."*

When he replied that he didn't accept the New Testament, I said, "Well, you know your Old Testament. In the Old Testament, the prophets of God were anointed with the Holy Spirit. We see a word of wisdom being given to one, and a word of knowledge to another. We see discerning of spirits and the gift of special faith in operation. We also see gifts of hearings working of miracles, and prophecy. This was the same Holy Spirit in manifestation, although no one spoke with the gift of tongues and interpreted in that dispensation.

Tongues and interpretation are distinctive to this dispensation."

The Jewish man wanted to see for himself these gifts of the Old Testament listed in the New Testament, so I opened my Bible and read it to him. And he was so impressed with seeing this gift of tongues and interpretation demonstrated, and then seeing it in the Bible that he promised to come back to the services. He wanted to learn more about the New Testament and Jesus the Messiah.

Some believe that all speaking in tongues is prayer and those who speak with tongues are always just praying. They believe the interpretation is really prophecy. But this was the gift of tongues and interpretation in manifestation. If I were only praying, this Jewish man would have known I was just praying because he knew the language. I wasn't praying, though. I was addressing the congregation by the demonstration of the gift of tongues with the interpretation.

Tongues for Edification

So we see that all tongues aren't prayer. But when the believer who is filled with the Holy Spirit speaks in tongues in his own private prayer life, this tongue is given to him to use in worship to God: *"He that speaketh in an unknown tongue edifieth himself..."* The word "edifieth" means to build oneself up. Greek scholars tell us that we have a word in our modern vernacular which is much closer to the original meaning than the word "edify." That word is "charge." We use the word "charge" in connection with charging a battery. A more literal translation would be, "He that speaks in an unknown tongue edifies, charges, or builds himself up like a battery."

This wonderful, supernatural means of spiritual edification is not for just a few of God's children: it is for every one of them. Also notice this "charging" or "building up" of oneself is neither *mental* nor *physical* edification. It is spiritual edification. Paul said, *"For if I pray in an unknown tongue, my spirit prayeth . . ."* (1 Cor. 14:14). *The Amplified Bible* adds, ". . . my spirit [by the Holy Spirit within me] prays, *but my mind is unproductive. . . ."* So speaking in tongues isn't mental edification; it is spiritual edification.

"For he that speaketh in an unknown tongue speaketh not unto men, but unto God: for no man understandeth him . . ." (1 Cor. 14:2). Here Paul isn't talking about diversities of tongues, or ministering in tongues in a public assembly; he is talking about the individual Spirit-filled believer employing the use of tongues in his prayer life. *". . . howbeit in the spirit he speaketh mysteries."*

When Cornelius and his household began to speak with tongues, the Bible says, *". . . they heard them speak with tongues, and MAGNIFY GOD"* (Acts 10:46). Speaking with tongues is the supernatural way to magnify God!

Fruit of the Spirit in the Believer

GALATIANS 5:22,23
22 But the fruit of the Spirit is love, joy, peace, longsuffering, gentleness, goodness, faith,
23 Meekness, temperance: against such there is no law.

Some argue, "But many people who speak with tongues don't have the fruit of the Spirit in their lives as they ought to have." However, the fruit Paul talks about in Galatians 5:22,23 is not the fruit of the baptism in the Holy Spirit at all; it is the fruit that should be in the life of every Christian as a result of being born again and experiencing the rebirth of the human *spirit*. The born-again human spirit produces the fruit, for Jesus said, *"I am the vine, ye are the branches . . ."* (John 15:5). The fruit grows on the branch just as the fruit grows in the life of the born-again, recreated child of God because of the life of Christ within.

The first fruit mentioned in Galatians 5:22 is love. Those who have received the baptism in the Holy

Spirit don't necessarily have any more love than other Christians do for the simple reason that Jesus said, *"By this shall all men know that ye are my disciples, if ye have love one to another"* (John 13:35). John said, *"We know that we have passed from death unto life, because we love the brethren"* (1 John 3:14). So love is fruit of the born-again human spirit; not fruit of the baptism in the Holy Spirit.

Another fruit listed in Galatians 5 is peace. I didn't have any more peace after I received the baptism in the Holy Spirit than I had before. *"Therefore being justified by faith, we have peace . . . ,"* Romans 5:1 says.

Baby Christians haven't produced and grown fruit yet. After all, we don't expect a baby tree to produce fruit. It takes time for fruit to grow. Yet that baby Christian can be filled with the Holy Spirit and have power in his life. The Corinthians were babes. Paul said, *"And I, brethren, could not speak unto you as unto spiritual but as unto carnal, even as unto babes in Christ"* (1 Cor. 3:1). Yet he said, *"ye come behind in no gift"* (1 Cor. 1:7).

Also notice that the fruit of the spirit is for HOLINESS — whereas the baptism in the Holy Spirit is for POWER.

You can be holy without having power, and you can have power without being very holy. Yet a combination of the two is best. I have seen people who are wonderful Christians and have marvelous fruit of the spirit, but there is no power in their lives. Then I know of others who are certainly powerhouses for God, but it is obvious that they need to grow a little more fruit in their lives.

It is wonderful what the Lord is doing in these days. God has given us a supernatural means of communicating with Him. He has given us a supernatural means of edifying ourselves; of building ourselves up spiritually. Are we taking advantage of it?

I am thoroughly convinced that if we would respond to the Holy Spirit, He would show us things to come, because He knows what is coming in the future, and He will equip us for what lies ahead.

Praying and speaking with tongues is one way we can be built up spiritually in order to be ready for whatever may come in the future.

＊

Memory Text:
"He that speaketh in an unknown tongue edifieth himself. . . ."
— 1 Cor. 14:4

Is It Scriptural To Tarry for The Holy Spirit? (Part 1)

Bible Texts: Acts 2:1-4; 8:5-8,12-17; 10:44-46;
19:1-3,6; 9:11,12,17

Central Truth: The infilling of the New Testament believers with the Holy Spirit should be our pattern today for receiving this blessed experience.

Tarrying has been thought by many to be a prerequisite to receiving the baptism in the Holy Spirit.

Certainly I believe in tarrying before the Lord. I believe in waiting and praying long and earnestly before God. Many times in our meetings we have waited five to six hours on the Lord in prayer.

Yet when I see people waiting and praying, crying out and agonizing to receive the Holy Spirit, it breaks my heart, because I know *this* "tarrying" isn't necessary.

Before the Day of Pentecost, Jesus said to His disciples, "*. . . but tarry ye in the city of Jerusalem, until ye be endued with power from on high*" (Luke 24:49).

Some have supposed this was the Bible formula for receiving the Holy

Spirit. If it were a formula for receiving, however, we would not have any right to take the word "Jerusalem" out of the text. Jesus told them not only to wait, or "tarry," but He said to wait in Jerusalem. Why didn't He say to tarry in Bethlehem? Why didn't He say to tarry in Jericho? Because it was necessary that they wait in Jerusalem, since the Church had to have its beginning there.

ACTS 2:1-4

1 And when the day of Pentecost was fully come, they were all with one accord in one place.

2 And suddenly there came a sound from heaven as of a rushing mighty wind, and it filled all the house where they were sitting.

3 And there appeared unto them cloven tongues like as of fire, and it sat upon each of them.

4 And they were all filled with the Holy Ghost, and began to speak with other tongues, as the Spirit gave them utterance.

The disciples were waiting for the Day of Pentecost to come; they were not waiting for an experience. They were not just waiting to be filled with the Holy Spirit. If that had been true, the Bible would have said, "When they were fully ready, the Holy Ghost came." But it doesn't say that. It says, *And when the day of Pentecost was fully come. . . ."* That is what they were waiting for — the day.

After the Day of Pentecost there is no record in the Bible anywhere that anyone ever waited, cried, agonized, sang, struggled, or tarried to be filled with the Holy Spirit!

Someone said, "I believe in receiving the Holy Spirit the old-fashioned way." I do, too. You can't get any more old-fashioned than the Acts of the Apostles. I propose that we look at Acts, see how they did it, and follow their example in getting people filled with the Holy Spirit.

Reading through the twenty-eight chapters of the Book of Acts, one who is not a Bible student might suppose he is reading something that had happened over a period of a few days, a few weeks, or even a few

years. However, the events in this book cover a number of years.

Eight years after the Day of Pentecost we see Philip carrying the Gospel to the people of Samaria.

Believers Filled in Samaria

ACTS 8:5-8

5 Then Philip went down to the city of Samaria, and preached Christ unto them.
6 And the people with one accord gave heed unto those things which Philip spake, hearing and seeing the miracles which he did.
7 For unclean spirits, crying with loud voice, came out of many that were possessed with them: and many taken with palsies, and that were lame, were healed.
8 And there was great joy in that city.

Joy is not necessarily a characteristic of being filled with the Holy Spirit. These people had great joy *before* they were filled with the Spirit. We can have joy before, and we can have joy afterwards. It is joyous to be saved. It is joyous to be healed. It is joyous to enjoy the blessings of God.

ACTS 8:12-17

12 But when they believed Philip preaching the things concerning the kingdom of God, and the name of Jesus Christ, they were baptized, both men and women.

13 Then Simon himself believed also: and when he was baptized, he continued with Philip, and wondered, beholding the miracles and signs which were done.

14 Now when the apostles which were at Jerusalem heard that Samaria had received the word of God, they sent unto them Peter and John:

15 Who, when they were come down, prayed for them, that they might receive the Holy Ghost:

16 (For as yet he was fallen upon none of them: only they were baptized in the name of the Lord Jesus.)

17 Then laid they their hands on them, and they received the Holy Ghost.

Philip had a glorious revival in Samaria. Hundreds of people must have been saved and scores healed. And all received the Holy Spirit. Notice, too, that they received without waiting, without praying, without agonizing, and without exception or disappointment.

Believers Filled in Cornelius' Household

Then ten years after the Day of Pentecost, the Bible tells us about Peter going to Cornelius' house to carry the Gospel.

In the tenth chapter of Acts, we see how an angel appeared to Cornelius and told him to send to Joppa and inquire in the house of a certain individual for Simon Peter, *"Who shall tell thee words, whereby thou and all thy house shall be saved"* (Acts 11: 14).

Until this time, neither Cornelius nor his household had been saved. They were Jewish proselytes. They didn't know Jesus had died. A person can't be saved without hearing the Gospel, so Peter preached to them. They believed and were born again *while Peter was preaching*, and they received the Holy Spirit and spoke in tongues *before* he had finished his message!

ACTS 10:44-46

44 While Peter yet spake these words, the Holy Ghost fell on all them which heard the word.

45 And they of the circumcision which believed were astonished, as many as came with Peter, because that on the Gentiles also was poured out the gift of the Holy Ghost.

46 For they heard them speak with tongues, and magnify God....

Notice that they were saved and filled with the Holy Spirit, speaking with tongues, without tarrying — without waiting, praising, or singing. We make a mistake by thinking things have to be done a certain way — except the Bible way. God doesn't have any cut-and-dried methods. While Peter was still preaching, these people received the

Holy Spirit. I have seen people receive the Holy Spirit while I was speaking too.

Believers Filled in Ephesus

Then twenty years after the Day of Pentecost, Paul journeyed to Ephesus. There he met some believers and introduced to them the Person of the Holy Spirit, as recorded in Acts 19:

ACTS 19:1-3,6
1 And it came to pass, that, while Apollos was at Corinth, Paul having passed through the upper coasts came to Ephesus: and finding certain disciples,
2 He said unto them, Have ye received the Holy Ghost since ye believed? And they said unto him, We have not so much as heard whether there be any Holy Ghost.
3 And he said unto them, Unto what then were ye baptized? And they said, Unto John's baptism . . . .
6 And when Paul had laid his hands upon them, the Holy Ghost came on them; and they spake with tongues, and prophesied.

As we see from the verses above, the believers at Ephesus never had heard about the Holy Spirit. But when Paul laid his hands on them, the Holy Spirit came upon them, and they spoke with tongues.

Every one of them — without waiting, without praising, and without tarrying — was filled with the Holy Spirit and spoke with other tongues as the Spirit of God gave them utterance.

Paul said to the Ephesians, *"Have ye received?"* He didn't say, "I have come here to pray that God would pour the Holy Spirit out on you." The Holy Spirit had already been poured out on the Day of Pentecost.

(We saw earlier, in Acts 8, that the apostles in Jerusalem sent Peter and John to Samaria to lay hands on Philip's converts to receive the Holy Spirit. They didn't send them to tarry and wait on God for the Holy Spirit.)

Paul's Infilling With the Spirit

Paul, who laid hands on the Ephesians, previously was known as Saul of Tarsus. The account of his experience of receiving the Holy Spirit is found in the ninth chapter of Acts:

ACTS 9:11,12,17
11 And the Lord said unto him, Arise, and go into the street which is called Straight, and enquire in the house of Judas for one called Saul of Tarsus: for, behold, he prayeth,
12 And hath seen in a vision a man named Ananias coming in, and putting his hand on him, that he might receive his sight. . . .
17 And Ananias went his way, and entered into the house; and putting his hands on him said, Brother Saul,

the Lord, even Jesus, that appeared unto thee in the way as thou camest, hath sent me, that thou mightest receive thy sight, and be filled with the Holy Ghost.

Saul, later known as Paul, received the Holy Spirit immediately. He didn't have to tarry or wait.

"But it doesn't say he spoke with tongues," someone might object. It is true it doesn't state this specifically right here, but Paul himself later said that he spoke with tongues: *"I thank my God, I speak with tongues more than ye all"* (1 Cor. 14:18). We know he didn't start talking with tongues *before* he got the Holy Spirit, so it shouldn't be too difficult to figure out when he started. He started when he received the Holy Spirit, just as the rest of us do, because tongues goes with that experience.

"But I remember those wonderful times I had of seeking God for several years before I was filled," someone once told me.

"Have you stopped seeking God?" I asked. "I remember that time I had last week seeking God. I remember that time today seeking God. I believe in seeking God and tarrying. Spirit-filled believers need to seek God just as much as people who are not filled."

"Yes, but I learned many lessons," a man said.

"You could have learned them a whole lot faster *with* the Holy Spirit than you did *without* Him," I said. "And isn't it true that the very thing you learned when you did get filled was that you didn't have to do all of that seeking?'"

He laughed and said, "You are exactly right. The first thing I said after I received was that if only someone had told me, I could have received years before."

We don't have to wait five years, five weeks, or even five minutes. The baptism in the Holy Spirit is a gift which every believer can receive *right now*!

✳

Memory Text:
"And, behold, I send the promise of my Father upon you: but tarry ye in the city of Jerusalem, until ye be endued with power from on high."
— Luke 24:49

Is It Scriptural To Tarry for The Holy Spirit? (Part 2)

Bible Texts: John 7:37-39; Luke 24:49; Acts 2:4

Central Truth: To receive the Holy Spirit, drink in of the Spirit of God, and utterance will be given to you.

In the last lesson, we read every recorded instance in the New Testament where people received the Holy Spirit over a twenty-year period.

We found that there is absolutely nothing in the Scriptures that even resembles what we would call a "tarrying meeting" in order for people to be filled with the Holy Spirit. In every instance where people sought the Holy Spirit, everyone received right away. Not one person went away disappointed. Therefore, if we taught this to our people today, they would receive in the same way — the Acts of the Apostles' way — the New Testament way.

I have had the baptism in the Holy Spirit since 1937, and I have never told anyone to wait or to tarry in order to receive the Holy Spirit. I have always told people, "Come and receive the Holy Spirit." And people everywhere have come and received the baptism in the Holy Spirit in my meetings.

Look to the Word, Not Experiences

The Early Church had no trial-and-error way of seeking the baptism in the Holy Spirit and not finding, or of coming and going away empty. We should be scriptural and tell people what the Word of God says. Too often people say what they *think*. They give their theory, or tell their *experience.* Paul, however, told Timothy, "Preach the Word." He didn't say, "Timothy, tell what you think about the Word." He didn't say, "Timothy, give your theory about such and such." The preaching of theory just produces doubt and unbelief. The facts of God's Word produce faith! That's why the Bible says, *"So then faith cometh by hearing, and hearing by the word of God"* (Rom. 10:17).

It is all right to refer to experience, but we must magnify the Word *above* experience. Everyone will have his own experience in the way he receives the baptism in the Holy Spirit, for experiences do vary. We will all speak with tongues, but some will have additional experiences. This does not mean, however, that one will have any more of the Holy Spirit than another.

Some have told of experiences in receiving the Holy Spirit of seeing a beam of light which seemed to come down through the ceiling; others have told of seeing a ball of fire. I have never seen any beam of light or ball of fire, but I am just as much filled with the Holy Spirit as anyone. I have the Bible evidence: I spoke with tongues.

I don't doubt that such experiences happen, but God didn't promise "experiences." If they happen, all right; but don't seek them. You do have a right, however, to seek to be filled with the Spirit and speak with tongues.

Many people also have unusual experiences when they are born again. For example, when Paul was converted, he saw a light and heard a voice. *"And as he journeyed, he came near Damascus: and suddenly there shined round about him a light from heaven: And he fell to the earth, and heard a voice saying unto him, Saul, Saul, why persecutest thou me?"* (Acts 9:3,4). However, when I was born again, I didn't see any light or hear any voice, but I am just as much born again as Paul was.

Paul never told people that they had to be converted in the same manner he was, or see a light or hear a voice as he did. He referred to this experience occasionally, but this is the way he taught people to be saved: *". . . If thou shalt confess with thy mouth the Lord Jesus, and shalt believe in thine heart that God hath raised him from the dead, thou shalt be saved"* (Rom. 10:9).

We thank God for Paul's experience in the way that he received the Holy Spirit, but we should not hold an experience up as the norm. *Magnify the Word, and let every man have his own experience.*

Too many times people have been given no instructions on the Bible way to receive the Holy Spirit. Or even worse, they receive *wrong* instructions. When they fail to receive, someone slaps them on the back and says, "Better luck next time." However, we don't receive from God by "luck"; we receive from God by faith.

Many have gone away discouraged. Those who should have received the Holy Spirit have been hindered from receiving. Many honest, sincere, intelligent people have been driven away by unscriptural practices. We must tell people *what the Word says.* "*The entrance of thy words giveth light . . .*" (Ps. 119:130). Proper instruction will save people hours of needless seeking.

'Come and Drink'

In the seventh chapter of John's Gospel, Jesus talks about receiving the Holy Spirit.

JOHN 7:37-39
**37 In the last day, that great day of the feast, Jesus stood and cried, saying, If any man thirst, let him come unto me, and DRINK.
38 He that believeth on me, as the scripture hath said, OUT of his belly shall flow RIVERS of living water.
39 (But this spake he of the SPIRIT, which they that believe on him should receive: for the Holy Ghost was not yet given; because that Jesus was not yet glorified.)**

In this passage, Jesus is talking about receiving the baptism in the Holy Spirit. These are rivers flowing out of the *believer.* But notice in John 4:14, Jesus said to the woman of Samaria "*. . . the water that I shall give him shall be IN him a WELL of*

water springing up into everlasting life." (v. 14). This is referring to salvation.

So in John 7:38 the reference is to RIVERS, and in John 4:14, the reference is to a WELL. It is obvious that these are two different experiences that Jesus is talking about. One — the well — is the blessing of the New Birth *in* you. It blesses *you.* It is the well of water in you springing up into everlasting life. It refers to salvation.

The other experience — the river is the baptism in the Holy Spirit — and that makes you a blessing to *others.* It is those rivers flowing *out* of you — it is the enduement of power Jesus promised in Luke 24 — and it is available to every believer.

LUKE 24:49
49 And, behold, I send the promise of my Father upon you: but tarry ye in the city of Jerusalem, until ye be endued with power from on high.

Also notice, in referring to receiving the baptism in the Holy Spirit, Jesus said, "Come and drink" — not "Come and shout, come and pray, or come and praise." He said, "Come and drink," not, "Come and then go away empty."

We make a mistake by not taking what Jesus said in the simplicity of the way He said it. Can you drink and talk at the same time? Have you

ever tried to drink water and talk?
Can you drink and sing or praise at
the same time?

The Holy Spirit is there to give
utterance, but you can't drink and
talk at the same time. So tell the
candidate to quit talking in English
and start drinking of the Spirit! Tell
him that *he* is to do the speaking in
tongues! The Holy Spirit will act on
his vocal organs, lips, and tongue,
and will put supernatural words on
his lips, but the candidate himself
must speak those words aloud.

The Holy Spirit gives the utterance, but man does the speaking.

ACTS 2:4
**4 And THEY were all filled with
the Holy Ghost, and [they] began to
speak with other tongues, as the
Spirit gave THEM utterance.**

"They" is the subject of the sen-
tence. *They* did the talking. The Holy
Spirit gave *them* the utterance.

Just drink in of the Spirit. Drink
until full; when you are full, the Holy
Spirit will give you the utterance in
tongues.

Someone might ask, "Do you
mean to insinuate there is no need to
tarry anymore?" No, I don't mean to
insinuate it; I mean to absolutely
state it! There is no need to tarry
anymore! Jesus said, "Come and
drink."

How long does it take you to
drink? Jesus said it is just as easy to
drink of the Spirit — that is, to be
filled with the Spirit — as it is to
drink water, or be filled with water.
On the other hand, drinking water
and being filled with water is something that *you* do, not something
that the water does. Drinking of the
Holy Spirit and being filled with the
Holy Spirit is something *you* do, not
something that the Holy Spirit does.

Infilling of the Holy Spirit:
A Gift

We can't do anything to merit the
Holy Spirit any more than we can do
anything to merit salvation. Babes in
Christ can receive the Holy Spirit
just as easily as mature Christians.
We don't receive the Holy Spirit
because we have graduated to some
marvelous degree of spirituality
beyond everyone else, and thus God
puts a seal on us saying we are perfect.

The Holy Spirit is a gift. *". . . ye
shall receive the GIFT of the Holy
Ghost"* (Acts 2:38). If you are born
again, you are ready to receive the
gift of the Holy Spirit. If you have to
do one thing to receive the Holy
Spirit, then receiving Him ceases to
be a gift and becomes a reward.

Some think I make it too easy for
people to receive the Holy Spirit. But
I wasn't the one who made it easy. I

wasn't the one who said, "Come and drink." It was Jesus. I wasn't the one who put receiving the Holy Spirit on a gift basis: It was God.

Someone said, "Yes, but I don't believe in 'railroading' people through to the Holy Spirit." If "railroading people through" means getting people filled with the Holy Spirit quickly, then does that same person believe in "railroading people through" to salvation? Does he believe in getting people saved as quickly as possible to insure that they don't die in the meantime and go to hell? Or if sick, does he believe in "railroading" people through to healing, or letting them linger awhile?

Salvation is a gift. Healing is a gift. The Holy Spirit is a gift. You can receive one gift just as quickly as you can receive the other!

Reading in the Acts of the Apostles, we see that the Early Church believed in getting people filled with the Holy Spirit as quickly as they did getting them saved or healed. (We saw this in our last lesson.) I not only believe in railroading people through; I believe in "jet-planing" them through!

Taking the Direct Route

Canaan's land is a type of the baptism in the Holy Spirit, and of our rights and privileges in Christ.

Some have thought it was a type of heaven. But Canaan couldn't be a type of heaven. There won't be any cities to conquer and battles to fight when we get to heaven. The last enemy — death — shall have been conquered. There won't be any enemies or giants in the land over there.

Israel came out of Egypt, which is a type of the world. The children of Israel were all baptized (going through the Red Sea was a type of water baptism). They all drank of Christ. (The rock out of which the water flowed, was Christ.) They could have gone right into Canaan, but because of unbelief and disobedience, they wandered in the wilderness for forty years. When they finally did go in, they took a detour.

If you want to detour before receiving the baptism in the Holy Spirit, you may. You may detour to the altar, detour by tarrying, detour a lot of ways. But you can also come directly into the baptism in the Holy Spirit. The door is open.

Another way to say it is this: If you want to go to a nearby city, you can go directly there. Or if you want to, you can go by way of St. Louis, on over to Memphis, down to Atlanta, back over to New Orleans, etc. You wouldn't have to, but you could. It is the same way with receiving the Holy Spirit. You can detour if you want to, but why not take the direct route and receive the Holy Spirit by faith?

Someone said, "More people have received the Holy Spirit after midnight than at any other time." My answer to that is, if they got the Holy Spirit *after* midnight it is because they didn't believe God *before* midnight. God is no different after midnight than He is before midnight.

Then there are those who warn, "Be careful about getting in the flesh." But you can't receive the baptism in the Holy Spirit any other way than in the flesh. Every person who ever got the Holy Spirit was in the flesh!

On the Day of Pentecost, Peter quoted Joel's prophecy, saying, *"And it shall come to pass afterward, that I will pour out my spirit upon all flesh . . ."* (Joel 2:28). Paul said, *"What? know ye not that your body* [flesh] *is the temple of the Holy Ghost . . .?"* (I Cor. 6:19).

To receive the Holy Spirit, open your being with a strong desire toward God. In simple faith breathe in, drink in, of the Spirit of God, and utterance will be given to you. If you are simple enough in faith and strong enough in courage, you can speak that utterance out right now. If you can drink water, you can drink of the Spirit right now. I am quoting good authority — the Lord Jesus Christ.

40

Ten Reasons Why Every Believer Should Speak in Tongues (Part 1)

Bible Texts: Acts 2:4; 1 Corinthians 14:4; John 14:16,17; Romans 8:26; Jude 20

Central Truth: Speaking in tongues is a flowing stream that should never dry up; it will enrich your life spiritually.

The Apostle Paul wrote and spoke at length on the subject of speaking in tongues. He apparently practiced what he preached, because he said, *"I thank my God, I speak with tongues more than ye all"* (1 Cor. 14:18).

I, too, thank God I speak in tongues regularly, and I wish every believer might know this blessing and source of power in his daily life.

The purpose of the next two lessons is to set forth major reasons why every Christian should speak in tongues, and to help Christians see the blessings that can be theirs through appropriating the power of the Holy Spirit daily.

Reason 1 — Tongues the Initial Sign

ACTS 2:4
4 And they were all filled with the Holy Ghost, and began to speak with other tongues, as the Spirit gave them utterance.

The Word of God teaches that when we are filled with the Holy Spirit we speak with other tongues as the Spirit of God gives utterance. Tongues is an initial evidence or sign of the baptism in the Holy Spirit. Therefore, the first reason people should speak with other tongues is because this is a supernatural evidence of the Spirit's indwelling.

In Acts 10, we read that the Jewish brethren who went with Peter to Cornelius' house were astonished when they saw that the gift of the Holy Spirit was poured out on the Gentiles. They thought it was just for the Jews.

How did these Jews *know* that Cornelius' household had received the gift of the Holy Spirit? *"For THEY HEARD THEM SPEAK with tongues, and magnify God"* (Acts 10:46).

Speaking in tongues was the supernatural sign which convinced them that the Gentiles had the same gift they had.

Reason 2 — Tongues for Spiritual Edification

1 CORINTHIANS 14:4
4 He that speaketh in an unknown tongue edifieth himself. . . .

In writing to the Church at Corinth, Paul encouraged believers to continue their practice of speaking with other tongues in worship and in their prayer lives for spiritual edification, or building up.

"For he that speaketh in an unknown tongue speaketh not unto men, but unto God: for no man understandeth him; howbeit in the spirit he speaketh mysteries" (1 Cor. 14:2). Moffatt's translation says that he speaks "divine secrets." Paul is saying here that God has given the Church a divine, supernatural means of communication with Himself!

In the 14th verse of this chapter Paul stated, *"For if I pray in an unknown tongue, my spirit prayeth, but my understanding is unfruitful."* Notice he said, "my spirit prayeth."

The Amplified Bible adds, "My spirit (by the Holy Spirit within me) prays."

God is a Spirit. When we pray in tongues, our spirit is in direct contact with God, who is a Spirit. We are talking to Him in a divine, supernatural means.

Howard Carter, who was general superintendent of the Assemblies of God in Great Britain for many years and founded the oldest Pentecostal Bible school in the world, said we must not forget that speaking with other tongues is not only the initial evidence of the Holy Spirit's infilling; it *also* is a continual experience for the rest of one's life. For what purpose? To assist us in the worship of God. Speaking in tongues is a flowing stream that should never dry up; it will enrich your life spiritually.

Reason 3 — Tongues Remind Us of the Spirit's Indwelling Presence

JOHN 14:16,17
16 And I will pray the Father, and he shall give you another Comforter, that he may abide with you for ever;
17 Even the Spirit of truth; whom the world cannot receive, because it seeth him not, neither knoweth him: but ye know him; for he dwelleth with you, and shall be in you.

Continuing to pray and worship God in tongues helps us to be ever conscious of His indwelling presence. If I can be conscious of the indwelling presence of the Holy Spirit every day, it is bound to affect the way I live.

A minister's 12-year-old daughter once lost her temper and was talking very rudely and hatefully to her mother. A visiting evangelist overheard the scene. When the girl looked up and saw him, knowing he had witnessed her tantrum, she was embarrassed and burst into tears.

The evangelist asked her if she was filled with the Holy Spirit. When she replied that she was, he reminded her that the Holy Spirit was in her. They had prayer together and she asked the Lord's forgiveness. While praying, she began to worship God in tongues.

When they were finished praying, the evangelist said to her, "There is one secret that will help you curb your temper. If you will pray and worship God every day in tongues, it will help you to be conscious of the indwelling presence of the Holy Spirit. If you remember He is in you, you won't act that way."

Some years later when the evangelist returned to preach at that church, the girl told him, "I have never forgotten what you said. Every day for the past few years I have prayed and worshipped God in tongues, and I have never lost my temper again."

Unfortunately, we all know people who have been filled with the Holy Spirit, yet they still lose their tempers and say and do things they shouldn't. This is only because they haven't been walking in the Spirit as they should.

It is so easy, when we are not conscious of His presence, to become irritated and frustrated. But if we will take the time to fellowship with Him, we can be conscious of His indwelling presence.

Reason 4 — Tongues Will Keep Our Prayers in Line With God's Will

ROMANS 8:26
26 Likewise the Spirit also helpeth our infirmities: for we know not what we should pray for as we ought: but the Spirit itself maketh intercession for us with groanings which cannot be uttered.

Speaking in tongues keeps selfishness out of our prayers. If I pray a prayer out of my own mind and out of my own thinking, it may be unscriptural. It may be selfish.

Too often our prayers are like the old farmer who always prayed, "God bless me, my wife, my son John, his wife — us four and no more."

In the scripture quoted above, Paul didn't say we don't know how to pray, because we do: We pray to the Father in the Name of the Lord Jesus Christ. This is the correct way to pray. But just because I know *how to pray* doesn't mean I know *what to pray for* as I should. Paul said, *". . . we know not what we should pray for as we ought: but the Spirit itself maketh intercession for us with groanings which cannot be uttered."*

P. C. Nelson said that the Greek here literally reads, "The Holy Ghost maketh intercession for us in groanings that cannot be uttered in articulate speech." (Articulate speech means our regular kind of speech.) He went on to point out that the Greek stresses that this not only includes groanings escaping our lips in prayer, but also praying in other tongues.

That agrees with what Paul said in First Corinthians 14:14: *"For if I pray in an unknown tongue, my spirit prayeth. . . ."* The Amplified Bible says, "My spirit (by the Holy Spirit within me) prays."

When you pray in tongues, it is your spirit praying by the Holy Spirit within you. It is the Holy Spirit within you giving you the utterance, and you are speaking it out of your spirit. *You* do the talking, *He* gives the utterance.

By that method the Holy Spirit is helping you pray according to the will of God, which is the way things should be prayed for. This isn't something that the Holy Spirit does apart from you. He doesn't groan or speak in tongues apart from you. Those groanings come from inside you and escape your lips.

The Holy Spirit is not going to do our praying for us. He is sent to dwell in us as a Helper and an Intercessor. He is not *responsible* for our prayer life; He is sent to *help* us to pray. Speaking with other tongues is praying *as the Spirit gives utterance.* It is Spirit-directed praying. It eliminates the possibility of selfishness in our prayers.

Many times when people have prayed out of their own minds, they have changed things that actually were not the will of God and were not best for them!

If God's people want something a certain way, even if it isn't best for them, or it isn't God's perfect will, He often will permit it. Remember, God did not want Israel to have a king, but they wanted one, so He permitted them to have one. But it was not His highest will.

Reason 5 — Praying in Tongues Stimulates Faith

JUDE 20
20 But ye, beloved, building up yourselves on your most holy faith, praying in the Holy Ghost.

The fifth reason every believer should speak with tongues is because it stimulates faith and helps us learn how to trust God more fully.

Because the Holy Spirit supernaturally directs the words I speak, *faith must be exercised to speak with tongues.* I don't know what the next word will be — I trust God for that. And trusting God in this area of life helps me trust Him in another.

There was a fine Christian woman in a country church I once pastored. She dearly loved the Lord, but she had an ulcerated stomach, and doctors feared it would lead to cancer. Her husband made good money, but he had spent everything he had on doctor bills. I sometimes stayed in their home.

Soon after this woman received the baptism in the Holy Spirit, I visited in their home again. I noticed that she was eating anything she wanted, whereas before she could eat only a little baby food and milk, and she had difficulty keeping even that on her stomach.

She told me, "I received not only the baptism in the Holy Spirit and spoke with other tongues, but I received my healing as well. I am perfectly well."

I have seen this happen many times. What is the connection? We know that receiving the baptism in the Holy Spirit doesn't heal us. However, speaking with tongues helps us learn how to trust God more fully.

In our next lesson we will study the remaining five reasons why every believer should speak in tongues.

Memory Text:
"I thank my God, I speak with tongues more than ye all."
— 1 Cor. 14:18

Ten Reasons Why Every Believer Should Speak in Tongues (Part 2)

Bible Texts: 1 Corinthians 14:28; Isaiah 28:11,12; 1 Corinthians 14:15-17; James 3:8

Central Truth: Yielding the tongue to the Holy Spirit to speak with other tongues is a giant step toward fully yielding all of our members to God.

Too few Christians today realize the potential power that is available to them through the Holy Spirit. In this lesson we will look at five more reasons why every believer should be filled with the Holy Spirit and speak in tongues.

Reason 6 — Praying in Tongues Keeps Us Free From Worldly Contamination

1 CORINTHIANS 14:28

28 But if there be no interpreter, let him keep silence in the church; and let him speak to himself, and to God.

The sixth reason every Christian should speak in tongues is because it is one way of keeping us free from contamination from ungodly, profane, and vulgar talk around us on the job or out in public.

Notice from the scripture above that we can speak with tongues to ourselves. It's different in a church service. Paul said regarding a church service, *"If any man speak in an unknown tongue, let it be by two, or at the most by three, and that by course, and let one interpret. But if there be no interpreter, let him keep silence in the church; and LET HIM SPEAK TO HIMSELF, AND TO GOD"* (1 Cor. 14:27,28).

If we do this in church, we can do it on the job. It won't disturb anyone. In a barber shop, for instance, if the men tell risque jokes, I just sit there and speak to myself and to God in tongues. Riding in a car, bus, or airplane, we can speak to ourselves and to God. On the job we can speak to ourselves and to God. Talking in tongues to yourself and to God is a means of keeping yourself free from contamination.

Reason 7 — Praying in Tongues Enables Us To Pray for the Unknown

The seventh reason every believer should speak in tongues is because it provides a way to pray about things no one thinks to pray about, or is even aware of.

We already know that the Holy Spirit helps us to pray because *". . . we know not what we should pray for as we ought . . ."* (Rom. 8:26). In addition, the Holy Spirit, who knows everything, can pray through us for things about which our natural mind knows nothing.

In 1956 when my wife and I were in California, I was awakened suddenly in the night. It was as if someone had laid his hand on me. I sat bolt upright in bed, my heart beating rapidly.

"Lord, what is the matter?" I asked. "I know something is wrong somewhere. Holy Spirit in me, You know everything. You are everywhere as well as within me. Whatever this is, You give me utterance."

I prayed in tongues for an hour and then I began to laugh and sing in tongues. (When praying this way, always continue praying until you have a note of praise. Then you will know that whatever it is you are praying about has been prayed through.)

I knew what I had been praying for had come to pass. I had the answer, so I went back to sleep.

I dreamed that I saw my younger brother become extremely ill in Louisiana. He had to be taken to the hospital in an ambulance. I dreamed that the doctor came out of his hospital room, pulled the door closed behind him, and told me he was dead.

I said, "No, doctor, he is not dead. The Lord told me he would live and not die." In the dream the doctor became very angry with me for doubting his professional ability. He took me into the room to see for myself that my brother was indeed dead.

Jerking the sheet from his face to prove that he was dead, the doctor saw that my brother was breathing and his eyes were open. Astonished, the doctor said, "Why, you knew something I didn't know. He is alive, isn't he?" I saw my brother rise up well and then the dream ended. I knew then that this was what I had been praying about.

Three months later when I saw my brother he said to me, "I nearly died while you were gone." I told him I knew all about the attack he had

had during the night and how he had been rushed to the hospital.

"How did you know?" he asked. I told him about my burden for prayer, followed by the dream.

He said, "That's exactly how it happened! They told me that for about forty minutes there at the hospital the doctor thought I was gone."

Praying in the Spirit provides a way for things to be prayed for that we wouldn't know anything about in the natural. The Holy Spirit, however, knows everything.

Reason 8 — Praying in Tongues Gives Spiritual Refreshing

ISAIAH 28:11,12
11 For with stammering lips and another tongue will he speak to this people.
12 To whom he said, This is the rest wherewith ye may cause the weary to rest; and this is the refreshing: yet they would not hear.

What is the rest, the refreshing, that the above scriptures refer to? Speaking in other tongues.

Sometimes the doctor recommends people take a rest-cure, but I know the best one in the world. Often when you take a vacation, you have to come home and rest before going back to work. But isn't it wonderful that we can take this "rest-cure" every day.

"... This is the rest ... this is the refreshing." We need this spiritual refreshing in these days of turmoil, perplexity, and anxiety.

Reason 9 — Tongues for Giving Thanks

1 CORINTHIANS 14:15-17
15 What is it then? I will pray with the spirit, and I will pray with the understanding also: I will sing with the spirit, and I will sing with the understanding also.
16 Else when thou shalt bless with the spirit, how shall he that occupieth the room of the unlearned say Amen at thy giving of thanks, seeing he understandeth not what thou sayest?
17 For thou verily givest thanks well, but the other is not edified.

When Paul said, *"he that occupieth the room of the unlearned"* in verse sixteen, he was referring to those who are unlearned in spiritual things.

If you invited me to dinner and said, "Please give thanks," and if I prayed in tongues, you wouldn't know what I said. You wouldn't be edified. Therefore, Paul said it would be better to pray with the understanding in such cases. If you do pray in tongues, you should interpret it so the unlearned will know what was said.

Notice Paul is saying that praying in tongues provides the most perfect way to pray and to give thanks, because he said, *"thou verily givest thanks well. . . ."* But in the presence of people who are unlearned, Paul said to pray with your understanding also so they can be edified; so they will understand what you say.

Reason 10 — Speaking in Tongues Brings the Tongue Under Subjection

JAMES 3:8
8 But the tongue can no man tame; it is an unruly evil, full of deadly poison.

Yielding your tongue to the Holy Spirit to speak with other tongues is a giant step toward fully yielding all of your members to God, because if you can yield this most unruly member, you can yield *any* member.

In conclusion, I want to point out that, while these ten reasons have dealt primarily with tongues in the individual believer's private life, it is also true that there is a public side to tongues.

First, when people receive the Holy Spirit publicly, they speak with other tongues as the Spirit gives utterance. Second, the Church is edified by speaking with other tongues in public assembly with interpretation.

Paul plainly stated that to prophesy is to speak unto men *"to edification, and exhortation and comfort"* (1 Cor. 14:3). But he said, " *. . . greater is he that prophesieth than he that speaketh with tongues, except he interpret. . ."* (1 Cor. 14:5). He is saying that tongues with interpretation is equivalent to prophecy. If he interprets, the one who is prophesying is not greater.

To illustrate, it takes two nickels to make a dime. However, two nickels are not the same as a ten-cent piece. Paul is saying that prophecy is like the dime, the ten-cent piece. Naturally, it would be better to have the dime than to have one nickel (speaking with tongues). But, if interpretation goes along with tongues, then the two together are the equivalent of prophecy.

Prophesying is *"speaking unto men to edification, and exhortation, and comfort."* Prophesying is not *preaching.* (However, sometimes there is an element of prophecy in preaching.)

If prophesying were preaching, you wouldn't have to make any preparation to preach. But you do have to study. Paul said, *"Study to shew thyself approved unto God . . ."* (2 Tim. 2:15).

You don't have to study to speak with tongues or to interpret. You don't have to study to prophesy. It comes by inspiration of the Spirit. Of course, when one is preaching under the inspiration of the Spirit and suddenly he says things he never thought of, that is inspiration and that is an element of prophecy.

Speaking with tongues plus interpretation edifies the Church. When used with the Word of God, speaking with tongues with interpretation convinces the unbeliever of the reality of the Presence of God, and often causes him to turn to God and be saved.

Jesus said, *"And these signs shall follow them that believe, In my name shall they cast out devils"* (Mark 16:17). That can be private or public.

"They shall lay hands on the sick, and they shall recover" (v. 18). That can be private or public.

Another sign is, *"They shall speak with new tongues"* (v. 17).

Of course, we don't want prolonged praying in tongues during a service, because unless there is an interpretation, people won't know what is said and will not be edified.

It is all right to pray in tongues as long as you like in the altar service, because you go there to get edified. If everyone is lifting his hands and praying sometime during the service, it's all right for you to pray in tongues. (I stand on the platform and pray that way in every service.)

But when the congregation ceases praying in tongues, I cease praying in tongues, too. The congregation wouldn't be edified if I went on and on. We need to know how to use what we have to the greatest advantage.

Memory Text:
"And these signs shall follow them that believe . . . they shall speak with new tongues."
— Mark 16:17

The Holy Spirit Within

Bible Texts: John 14:16,17; 1 Corinthians 3:16; 6:19; 2 Corinthians 6:16; 1 John 4:4

Central Truth: Christ's purpose in sending the Holy Spirit was so that He, a divine Personality, might live in us.

In this lesson we will deal further with the subject of the indwelling presence of the Holy Spirit in the Spirit-filled believer.

There is no need for any believer ever to feel comfortless, bereaved, or forlorn. Christ's purpose in sending the Holy Spirit was that He, a divine Personality, might come to live in us and be in us.

The Holy Spirit, Our Helper

JOHN 14:16,17

16 And I will pray the Father, and he shall give you another Comforter, that he may abide with you for ever;
17 Even the Spirit of truth; whom the world cannot receive, because it seeth him not, neither knoweth him: but ye know him; for he dwelleth with you, and shall be in you.

The Amplified Bible reads, "And I will ask the Father, and He will give you another Comforter (Counselor, Helper, Intercessor, Advocate, Strengthener and Standby) that He may remain with you forever, The Spirit of Truth, Whom the world cannot receive (welcome, take to its heart), because it does not see Him, nor know and recognize Him. But you know and recognize Him, for He lives with you [constantly] and will be in you. I will not leave you orphans — comfortless, desolate, bereaved, forlorn, helpless — I will come [back] to you" (John 14:16-18).

Notice Jesus said the Holy Spirit would be a Comforter, Counselor, Helper, Intercessor, Advocate, Strengthener, and Standby. We don't need anything more than that. But often we have been so concerned

53

about receiving the baptism in the Holy Spirit through a natural, outward experience or feeling of ecstasy that we have missed the reality of what the Holy Spirit came to do in us.

Often when we need help we run here and there, trying to find someone to pray for us. We forget we have a Helper on the inside. We don't have to pray for a helper; we already have a Helper in us!

1 CORINTHIANS 3:16

16 Know ye not that ye are the temple of God, and that the Spirit of God dwelleth in you?

The Amplified translation of this verse reads, "Do you not discern and understand that you [the whole church at Corinth] are God's temple (His sanctuary), and that God's Spirit has His permanent dwelling in you — to be at home in you [collectively as a church and also individually]?"

1 CORINTHIANS 6:19

19 What? know ye not that your body is the temple of the Holy Ghost which is in you, which ye have of God, and ye are not your own?

The Amplified version of this scripture reads, "Do you not know that your body is the temple — the very sanctuary — of the Holy Spirit Who lives within you, Whom you have received [as a Gift] from God? You are not your own."

2 CORINTHIANS 6:16

16 And what agreement hath the temple of God with idols? for ye are the temple of the living God; as God hath said, I will dwell in them, and walk in them; and I will be their God, and they shall be my people.

Again, *The Amplified* translation of this verse reads, "What agreement [can there be between] a temple of God and idols? For we are the temple of the living God; even as God said, I will dwell in and with and among them and will walk in and with and among them, and I will be their God, and they shall be My people."

1 JOHN 4:4

4 Ye are of God, little children, and have overcome them: because greater is he that is in you, than he that is in the world.

Who is the "he" that is in the world? (Satan, the god of this world.) But there is a Greater One in you! God Himself in the Person of the Holy Spirit is in the born-again, Spirit-filled believer.

All that God could possibly be and do for you, the Holy Spirit is to you and for you. This Greater One who is referred to is the Holy Spirit, who is in you. He is greater than he who is in the world.

Instead of believing what the Bible *says*, too many people believe only what they *feel*. When they received the Holy Spirit, they felt wonderful. Later they said, "I had a marvelous experience, but He must have left me, because I don't feel now as I did then." However, Jesus said, "*. . . that he may abide with you for ever.*"

The Holy Spirit didn't come as a guest to stay for just a few days. He didn't come on a vacation. He came to dwell in you — to be at home in you! *The Holy Spirit's home in this life is in your body.*

People talk about the outward manifestation and miss the reality of His indwelling presence. We should be conscious of His presence during every waking moment!

The Holy Spirit, Our Guide

The Holy Spirit also is our Guide. "*Howbeit when he, the Spirit of truth, is come, he will guide you into all truth . . .*" (John 16:13). Not only will He guide us into all truth, but as Jesus said, "*Thy word is truth.*" He will guide us into the truth of God's Word.

He also will guide us in life. "*For as many as are led by the Spirit of God, they are the sons of God*" (Rom. 8:14).

No one can be guided or led without placing himself in the hands of the guide. It is needless to pray, "Lord, guide me, give me directions," unless we are willing to allow ourselves to be guided.

When we tour some place that has a guide available, if we don't follow the guide, there will be much that we will not understand, because the guide can explain it. Certainly no one would want to go through Carlsbad Caverns without a guide. It is pitch black inside those caverns. But the guide knows right where to turn on the lights. (Thank God, the Holy Spirit knows right where to turn on the lights too!) We never would get out of the caverns if we failed to follow the guide.

That is the reason many people have gotten into such a mess in life — they are not following the Guide. The Holy Spirit will guide us, but we have to put ourselves into His hands.

During the many years I traveled on the evangelistic field, leaving my wife and small children at home, I depended upon my Guide, the Holy Spirit. He always warned me ahead of time of a need in my family. And although I had no communication with my sister and brothers other than in the Spirit, I always knew when one of the family was sick.

Once while ministering in Oregon, I was very burdened in prayer.

The Holy Spirit showed me that my older brother was in difficulty, but he would be all right.

I told my wife, "The doctors will think his condition is very serious and, from the natural, it is serious, but he will be all right."

In just a few hours a long-distance call came from my sister. She was almost in hysterics as she said, "Our brother has had an accident and has broken his back. He is in very serious condition. What are we going to do?"

Thank God, I was able to tell her, "I already have *inside* information on this. He is not as bad as they think he is. He will be all right. Don't fret about it."

Later the doctors said to him, "We don't understand it. The X-rays show that your back is broken. Why you aren't paralyzed we don't know." I knew, however. My brother was in Kansas, but there was an Intercessor in me in Oregon — the Holy Spirit.

If space permitted, I could tell of experience after experience. But let me say that the Holy Spirit is not in me to help me just because I am a preacher. He is in you to help you too. If you will learn to listen to Him and look to Him, He will guide you. When you have guidance, you can be prepared ahead of time. He will guide you into all truth, and He also will guide you and lead you in life.

The Holy Spirit, Our Teacher

Jesus said, ". . . *he shall not speak of himself; but whatsoever he shall hear, that shall he speak. . . .*" What shall He speak? What He hears God say. Not only will He speak whatever He hears, but ". . . *he will shew you things to come*" (John 16:13).

John 15:26 says, "*But when the Comforter is come, whom I will send unto you from the Father, even the Spirit of truth, which proceedeth from the Father, he shall testify of me.*" Notice again John 16:14, "*He shall glorify me: for he shall receive of mine, and shall shew it unto you.*" In other words, the Holy Spirit will make Jesus real to you.

"*But the Comforter, which is the Holy Ghost, whom the Father will send in my name, he shall teach you all things, and bring all things to your remembrance, whatsoever I have said unto you*" (John 14:26).

Some people say, "I have a poor memory and just can't remember things. I can't remember scriptures." I tell them, "Why don't you quit trying to remember and look to Him and expect Him to bring them to your remembrance." It is one thing to do something mentally yourself and it's another thing to trust the Holy Spirit who is in you. He is everything in you the Word says He is. He'll do everything in us the Word says He will do. He will be everything in us the Word says He will be.

Smith Wigglesworth said in *Ever Increasing Faith*, "I am a thousand times bigger on the inside than I am on the outside." To illustrate this he told of an experience in England when he was asked to pray for the insane daughter of an elderly couple.

The parents led him to an upstairs room, pushed open the door and stepped back, motioning him to enter. Inside, he saw the frail young woman lying on the floor. She was so violent she was being held down by five men.

As Wigglesworth entered the room, she screamed, eyes blazing, "We are many. You can't cast us out."

Quietly he said, "Jesus can." He remembered the Bible said, *"greater is he that is in you"* and that he was a thousand times bigger on the inside than on the outside. He dared to believe that God was within him. He said to the woman, "Jesus can. And out you come in the Name of the Lord Jesus Christ." Thirty-seven devils came out and the woman's mind was completely restored. She dressed and went downstairs later in the day to eat the evening meal with her family.

Someone asked Wigglesworth, "What is your secret? What great place of spirituality have you attained?"

His answer was, "All I did was to remember that greater is He that is in me than he that is in the world. Dare to act on that scripture."

John was writing to laymen when he said, *"Ye are of God, little children, and have overcome them: because greater is he that is in you, than he that is in the world."*

You are not left helpless. The Greater One is in you. You have authority over the devil!

✳

Memory Text:
". . . greater is he that is in you, than he that is in the world."
— 1 John 4:4

Seven Steps To Receiving The Holy Spirit (Part 1)

Bible Texts: Acts 2:4; 10:46; 19:6;
1 Corinthians 14:2,4,5,14,15,18,27

Central Truth: God gave the gift of the Holy Spirit on the Day of Pentecost. All the believer must do now is receive God's gift.

These next two lessons have a twofold purpose: to help those who have not yet received the infilling of the Holy Spirit, and to help Spirit-filled believers pray with those seeking to receive this experience.

In these lessons I will share seven steps any layman can take to help anyone get filled with the Holy Spirit without waiting and without tarrying. I have successfully used these seven steps for years in my meetings across the country.

Step 1: The Gift Has Already Been Given

Help the candidate see that *God has already given the Holy Spirit to believers, and it is now up to the individual to receive the gift.* Above all, help him see that he is not to beg

God to fill him with the Holy Spirit! God promised to send His Holy Spirit to believers and this promise was fulfilled on the Day of Pentecost. The Holy Spirit came then. He has been here ever since, and people have *received* the infilling of the Holy Spirit ever since.

For example, nineteen or twenty years after the Day of Pentecost, we read in Acts 19, "*. . . Paul having passed through the upper coasts came to Ephesus: and finding certain disciples, He said unto them, Have ye RECEIVED the Holy Ghost since ye believed?*" (vv. 1,2). Notice Paul didn't say, "Has God *given* you the Holy Ghost?" He said, "*Have ye RECEIVED the Holy Ghost . . . ?*"

"*And they said unto him, We have not so much as heard whether there be any Holy Ghost . . . And when*

59

Paul had laid his hands upon them, the Holy Ghost came on them . . ." (vv. 2,6). We see that Paul didn't teach these believers to pray that God would *give* them the Holy Spirit. And notice that WHEN hands were laid upon these believers they RECEIVED the Holy Spirit: *"And WHEN Paul had laid his hands upon them, the Holy Ghost came on them; and THEY SPAKE WITH TONGUES, and prophesied"* (v. 6).

Another example of believers receiving the Holy Spirit without waiting and without tarrying, occurs in the eighth chapter of Acts — eight years after the Day of Pentecost: *"Now when the apostles which were at Jerusalem heard that Samaria had received the word of God, they sent unto them Peter and John: Who, when they were come down, prayed for them, that they might RECEIVE the Holy Ghost"* (Acts 8:14,15). Peter and John didn't pray that God would *give* the Samaritans the Holy Spirit; they prayed that the Samaritans might *receive* the Holy Spirit.

We see in verse seventeen, *"Then laid they their hands on them, and they RECEIVED the Holy Ghost."* God hasn't *given* the Holy Spirit to anyone since the Day of Pentecost. That's the day He was *given* to the Church. Since then believers have *received* Him. The Holy Spirit is already here for believers to receive.

Step 2: Salvation Is the Only Prerequisite

Help the person see that anyone who is saved is ready to receive the Holy Spirit. *"Now when they* [the multitude that had gathered after the 120 had received the Holy Spirit and to whom Peter preached, quoting Joel's prophecy] *heard this, they were pricked in their heart, and said unto Peter and to the rest of the apostles, Men and brethren, what shall we do? Then Peter said unto them, Repent, and be baptized every one of you in the name of Jesus Christ for the remission of sins, and ye shall receive the gift of the Holy Ghost"* (Acts 2:37,38). Anyone who is saved is ready to receive the gift of the Holy Spirit *now*.

Some people think there are certain things they have to do to qualify to receive the baptism in the Holy Spirit. However, if a person is saved, he couldn't possibly be any cleaner than he is at that moment. The blood of Jesus Christ cleanses us from all sin. We believe that saved people go to heaven when they die. If they are good enough to go to heaven, they are good enough to have a little bit of heaven in them!

Some people think that they have to follow certain standards of dress in order to receive the Holy Spirit. Others have the mistaken idea that they have to court God's favor to get

Him to do something for them. But the Bible says all we have to do is be saved and walk in the light of salvation. (A person who is out of fellowship, of course, would have to come back into fellowship with God.)

Some people have imagined that one has to be perfect before he can receive the Holy Spirit. However, even the great apostle Paul himself said, *"Not as though I had already attained, either were already perfect. . . . I count not myself to have apprehended: but this one thing I do, forgetting those things which are behind, and reaching forth unto those things which are before, I press toward the mark for the prize of the high calling of God in Christ Jesus"* (Phil. 3:12,13).

If you could do everything you ought to do and be everything you ought to be without the Holy Spirit, what would you need Him for? If you can do it yourself, why would you need Him?

Carnal Christians *can* be filled with the Holy Spirit. The Bible said the Corinthian Christians were carnal, yet Paul said of them, *". . . ye come behind in no gift . . ."* (1 Cor. 1:7). He was not endorsing carnality, to be sure. He was trying to get them to grow up in God and outgrow carnality!

Baby Christians can be filled with the Holy Spirit. Certainly carnal Christians and baby Christians need to be filled *more* than anyone, because they will then receive power that will help them, if they walk in the light of it, to outgrow these things. So, if a person is saved, he is ready to receive the Holy Spirit.

Step 3: Laying on of Hands

I always tell people that when I lay hands on them, they are to receive the Holy Spirit. Anyone can lay hands on another in faith, for God honors faith. However, there is a ministry of laying on of hands, and some are used along this line more than others. But anyone could lay their hands on a person as a contact of faith and tell him, "This is the minute — right now — you are to receive the Holy Spirit." *The Holy Spirit is then received by faith.*

Step 4: Expect To Speak in Tongues

Tell the candidate what to expect. If we don't, he may not know what is happening when the Holy Spirit moves on him. Tell him that he is to *expect* the Holy Spirit to move upon his vocal chords and to put supernatural words on his lips which he is to speak out in cooperation with the Holy Spirit. Remember, the person himself must do the speaking — he must lift his voice by an act of his will. The Holy Spirit gives the utterance, but the person does the talking.

ACTS 2:4
4 And THEY ... BEGAN TO SPEAK with other tongues, as the Spirit gave them utterance.

ACTS 10:46
46 For they heard THEM SPEAK with tongues, and magnify God.

ACTS 19:6
6 And when Paul had laid his hands upon them, the Holy Ghost came on them; and THEY SPAKE with tongues, and prophesied.

1 CORINTHIANS 14:2,4,5,14,15,18,27
2 FOR HE THAT SPEAKETH in an unknown tongue speaketh not unto men, but unto God: for no man understandeth him; howbeit in the spirit HE SPEAKETH mysteries....
4 HE THAT SPEAKETH in an unknown tongue edifieth himself....
5 I would that YE ALL SPEAK with tongues....
14 For if I PRAY in an unknown tongue, my spirit prayeth, but my understanding is unfruitful.
15 What is it then? I WILL PRAY with the spirit, and I will pray with the understanding....
18 I thank my God, I SPEAK with tongues more than ye all....
27 If any MAN SPEAK in an unknown tongue, let it be by two, or at the most by three, and that by course; and let one interpret.

Notice that every one of these scriptures shows that in receiving the Holy Spirit (as well as after receiving the Holy Spirit), or in praying in tongues, or in ministering tongues in the public assembly, it is always man who does the talking.

When I tell this to people who have been seeking the Holy Spirit for thirty or forty years, they often look at me in amazement and say, "If I had known that, I could have been speaking in tongues for the last thirty years. I had the urge; I had the prompting. It was all I could do sometimes to keep from talking in tongues, but I was waiting for the Holy Spirit to come and take my tongue over."

Some people think that it is as if one might swallow a small radio, and when God gets ready, He turns it on and it starts talking automatically! However, the Holy Spirit gives *you* the utterance, and *you* do the talking.

When the Spirit of God is moving on your tongue and lips, *you must* lift *your* voice and put sound to it. You are then cooperating with the Holy Spirit and you will find yourself speaking with tongues!

✳

Memory Text:
"I would that ye all spake with tongues. . . ."
— 1 Cor. 14:5

Seven Steps To Receiving The Holy Spirit (Part 2)

Bible Text: Luke 11:11-13

Central Truth: If you will act on God's Word, He will honor His Word, and you will receive the Holy Spirit.

We learned in the last lesson that in order to help believers receive the infilling of the Holy Spirit they must realize that:

1. God has already given the Holy Spirit to believers, and it is up to the individual to receive this gift.

2. Salvation is the only prerequisite for the infilling of the Holy Spirit.

3. Laying on of hands can be an important contact of faith.

4. The believer should expect to speak in tongues.

Let us now look at three more important steps to receiving this blessed infilling of the Holy Spirit.

Step 5: The Child of God Need Not Fear Receiving Something False

Some people fear that they might receive something false or counter-feit when they seek the infilling of the Holy Spirit. I have heard people say, "There is a wrong spirit as well as a right spirit. I want to get the right Spirit." To these people I point out this scripture:

LUKE 11:11-13

11 If a son shall ask bread of any of you that is a father, will he give him a stone? or if he ask a fish, will he for a fish give him a serpent?

12 Or if he shall ask an egg, will he offer him a scorpion?

13 If ye then, being evil, know how to give good gifts unto your children: how much more shall your heavenly Father give the Holy Spirit to them that ask him?

Jesus was saying here, "If your child asked you for bread, would you give him a stone? If your child asked for a fish would you give him a serpent? If your child asked you for an egg, would you offer him a scorpion?" No, you wouldn't.

"If ye then, being evil know how to give good gifts unto your children: how much more shall your heavenly Father give the Holy Spirit to them that ask him?" We can be assured that God will not give His children a counterfeit when they ask Him for the Holy Spirit.

It is a different thing entirely, of course, when an unsaved person is seeking the Holy Spirit. But if a person is a child of God, he will not receive an evil spirit.

Notice that the expressions "serpent" and "scorpion" were also used in Luke 10:19. *"Behold, I give unto you power to tread on serpents and scorpions, and over all the power of the enemy. . . ."* Jesus used the terms "serpents" and "scorpions" to refer to evil spirits. He said you are not going to get a "serpent" or a "scorpion." If you are a child of God and you come to your heavenly Father seeking the Holy Spirit, that is what you are going to receive.

When I have given these scriptures to those who have been misled by false teachers, I have seen them immediately begin to speak with tongues. Later they told me, "If I had known this, I could have been speaking with tongues and could have

known the fullness of the Spirit for many years. But I was afraid that I might get a wrong spirit." We can be relieved of our fears through the Word of God.

Step 6: Receive the Holy Spirit and Speak the Language He Gives

Tell the candidate to open his mouth and breathe in as deeply as possible. At the same time he should tell God in his heart, "I am receiving the Holy Spirit right now by faith."

I like to absolutely insist that candidates speak not one word of their natural language. Then, when the Holy Spirit begins to move upon them, I tell them to lift their voice and speak out whatever sounds seem easy to make, regardless of how they sound. I tell them to begin to speak the words and language the Spirit gives them, praising God with those supernatural words until a clear, free language comes. When that person can hear himself speak in tongues, he will have assurance and confidence that he has received the Holy Spirit.

In John 7:37-39, Jesus said to come and drink. *"In the last day, that great day of the feast, Jesus stood and cited, saying, If any man thirst, let him come unto me, and DRINK. He that believeth on me, as the scripture hath said, out of his belly shall*

64

flow rivers of living water. (But this spake he of the Spirit, which they that believe on him should receive: for the Holy Ghost was not yet given; because that Jesus was not yet glorified.)"

Receiving the Holy Spirit, Jesus said, is like drinking water; the same principle is involved. No one can drink with his mouth shut!

Also, no one can *drink* and *talk* at the same time.

I have seen people come to receive with their mouths open. I haven't seen anyone who would open his mouth wide, who didn't receive instantly. Once I saw five businessmen walking down the aisle with their mouths wide open, and they were all filled with the Holy Spirit. Jesus said, "Come and drink." If you will act on God's Word, He will honor His Word, and you will receive.

Step 7: No Confusing Crowd Should Gather Around the Candidate

I like to have a few workers whom I have specially instructed to help seekers, because people are often slow about yielding to the Spirit, and someone else is able to lead them and help them yield. (Sometimes when going swimming it is hard to get some people to go into the water, but if you go in and swim around, telling them how good it is,

they will come on in.) Sometimes your being there talking in tongues will encourage the seekers to follow you on into the baptism in the Holy Spirit.

Don't crowd around candidates who are seeking the Holy Spirit with everyone trying to give instructions at the same time. This will only bring confusion. Let just one person teach them how to yield to the Spirit.

If you are among those praying with the seekers, do one of two things: If you pray aloud, pray in tongues. Otherwise, pray quietly. If you pray in English, candidates will hear what you are saying, and this will get their minds on you. Many times people will be hindered from yielding to God because they are listening to what those around them are saying.

I have been in Full Gospel circles for half a century, and I have seen nearly everything you can mention — and a lot of things I hate to mention.

I have seen dear people at the altar seeking to be filled with the Holy Spirit, while someone on one side of them yells in one ear, "Hold on, brother, hold on!" Someone else might be hollering in the other ear, "Turn loose, brother, turn loose." Someone kneeling right behind them would be beating them on the back, yelling, "Let go, brother, let go!"

65

Then someone sitting right in front of them shouts, "Die out, brother, die out!" at the top of his voice.

Not because of it, but *in spite* of it, multitudes have received. But, at the same time, many honest and sincere people have been driven away. We will see more filled with the Holy Spirit if we follow scriptural practices.

By following the seven steps which we have outlined in these two lessons, you will be able to help people receive the Holy Spirit. And you will feel personally blessed and rewarded for your part in their receiving this wonderful infilling of God's power.

Memory Text:
*"Ask ye of the Lord rain
in the time of the
latter rain. . . ."*
— Zech. 10:1

ABOUT THE AUTHOR

The ministry of Kenneth E. Hagin has spanned more than 60 years since God miraculously healed him of a deformed heart and incurable blood disease at the age of 17. Today the scope of Kenneth Hagin Ministries is worldwide. The ministry's radio program, "Faith Seminar of the Air," is heard coast to coast in the U. S. and reaches more than 100 nations. Other outreaches include: *The Word of Faith*, a free monthly magazine; crusades, conducted nationwide; RHEMA Correspondence Bible School; RHEMA Bible Training Center; RHEMA Alumni Association and RHEMA Ministerial Association International; and a prison ministry.

The Word of Faith

The Word of Faith is a full-color monthly magazine with faith-building teaching articles by Rev. Kenneth E. Hagin and Rev. Kenneth Hagin Jr.

The Word of Faith also includes encouraging true-life stories of Christians overcoming circumstances through God's Word, and information on the various outreaches of Kenneth Hagin Ministries and RHEMA Bible Church.

To receive a free subscription to *The Word of Faith*, call:

1-888-28-FAITH — Offer #603

(1-888-283-2484)

To use our Internet address:
http://www.rhema.org

BOOK FAVORITES

ANOTHER LOOK AT FAITH

Kenneth Hagin Jr. • Item #733

This book focuses on what faith is not, thus answering common misunderstandings of what it means to live by faith.

THE BELIEVER'S AUTHORITY

Kenneth E. Hagin • Item #406

This powerful book provides excellent insight into the authority that rightfully belongs to every believer in Christ!

BLESSED IS . . . Untying the 'NOTS' That Hinder Your Blessing!

Kenneth Hagin Jr. • Item #736

This book creatively teaches believers from Psalm 1 what *not* to do in order to be blessed by God and receive His richest and best!

DON'T QUIT! YOUR FAITH WILL SEE YOU THROUGH

Kenneth Hagin Jr. • Item #724

Learn how you can develop faith that won't quit and come out of tests or trials victoriously.

FAITH FOOD DEVOTIONS

Kenneth E. Hagin • Item #045

Rev. Kenneth E. Hagin's beautiful, hardcover devotional book, *Faith Food Devotions*, contains 365 bite-sized teachings and faith-filled confessions for triumphant Christian living every day of the year!

FOLLOWING GOD'S PLAN FOR YOUR LIFE

Kenneth E. Hagin • Item #519

It's up to individual Christians to fulfill the divine purpose that God ordained for their lives before the beginning of time. This book can help believers stay on the course God has set before them!

GOD'S WORD: A Never-Failing Remedy

Kenneth E. Hagin • Item #526

The never-failing remedy for every adversity of life can be found in the pages of God's holy written Word! And when you act on the Word, it truly becomes a never-failing remedy!

THE HEALING ANOINTING

Kenneth E. Hagin • Item #527

This dynamic book explores the operation of God's powerful anointing in divine healing.

HEALING: Forever Settled

Kenneth Hagin Jr. • Item #723

The primary question among believers is whether it's God's will to heal people today. Healing is a forever-settled subject because God's Word is forever settled!

HOW TO LIVE WORRY-FREE

Kenneth Hagin Jr. • Item #735

Sound teaching from God's Word is combined with practical insights to illustrate the perils of worry and to help guide the believer into the peace of God.

HOW YOU CAN BE LED BY THE SPIRIT OF GOD

Kenneth E. Hagin • Item #513

These step-by-step guidelines based on the Scriptures can help Christians avoid spiritual pitfalls and follow the Spirit of God in every area of life.

IT'S YOUR MOVE!

Kenneth Hagin Jr. • Item #730

Move out of the arena of discouragement and despair and into the arena of God's blessings that are yours in Christ.

RHEMA
Bible Training Center

Providing Skilled Laborers for the End-Time Harvest!

Do you desire —

- to find and effectively fulfill God's plan for your life?
- to know how to "rightly divide the Word of truth"?
- to learn how to follow and flow with the Spirit of God?
- to run your God-given race with excellence and integrity?
- to become not only a laborer but a *skilled* laborer?

If so, then RHEMA Bible Training Center is here for you!

For a free video and full-color catalog, call:

1-888-28-FAITH — Offer #602
(1-888-283-2484)

To use our Internet address:
http://www.rhema.org

RHEMA Bible Training Center admits students of any race, color, or ethnic origin.

A YEAR AT THE LORD'S TABLE

RHEMA Bible Church Pastoral Staff • Item #SRB6

This manual includes a sermon outline for each of its twelve audiotaped messages taught by the RHEMA Bible Church pastoral staff to celebrate the redemptive work of Christ through the Communion service.

GETTING STARTED IN THE MINISTRY

2-Cassette Tape Series • Item #SRB1

In this series, a CPA and an attorney-at-law address the business and legal considerations involved in establishing a church or ministry. This series is a wise investment for anyone starting out in the ministry.

THE MINISTRY OF HELPS

Item #955

This quick-reference guide covers many of the major aspects of the ministry of helps. Subjects include: Developing Prayer Groups in the Church, The Church Music Program, and 14 other pertinent topics!

MISSIONARY STRATEGIES

Item #957

Believers called to the mission field will find this book a tremendous aid in preparing to pursue God's call. *Missionary Strategies* will also help those who have a heart for missions to better understand and respond to a missionary's unique needs.

THE PASTORAL MINISTRY

Item #954

This comprehensive manual contains practical information regarding issues that relate to churches. Topics include: Effective Pastoring, Church Insurance Needs, Church Legalities, and many more.

PIONEERING STRATEGIES

Item #956

This book was written by ordained RHEMA Ministerial Association International pastors who have successfully pioneered churches. *Pioneering Strategies* gives ministers practical business information, inspiration, and encouragement to help them establish a new work!

MUSIC FAVORITES

HE'LL DO IT AGAIN!
RHEMA Singers & Band
Cassette: MS07-C • Compact Disc: MS07-CD

INSTRUMENTAL PRAISE
RHEMA Singers & Band
Cassette: MS09-C • Compact Disc: MS09-CD

LOOK WHAT THE LORD HAS DONE!
RHEMA Singers & Band
Cassette: MS10-C • Compact Disc: MS10-CD

THE REASON FOR IT ALL (Christmas)
RHEMA Singers & Band
Cassette: MS08-C • Compact Disc: MS08-CD

TRUST AND OBEY
Joel Siegel
Cassette: MS11-C • Compact Disc: MS11-CD

*RHEMA Singers & Band (RS&B) has developed
22 accompaniment trax for your singing pleasure.
Call for listings.*